We the People...

do ordain and establish this
Constitution for the United States of America

Student Text

Level I

Center for Civic Education 5146 Douglas Fir Road ● Calabasas, CA 91302 ● (818) 340-9320

Prepared for the
National Bicentennial Competition on the
Constitution and Bill of Rights

Directed by the
Center for Civic Education
and
Cosponsored by the
Commission on the Bicentennial of the
United States Constitution

Cover: "Jolly Flatboatmen," 1848, George Caleb Bingham
Daniel J. Terra Collection
Terra Museum of American Art, Chicago

ISBN 0-89818-114-3

Acknowledgments

The following staff and consultants have contributed to the development of this text.

Editorial Directors
Charles N. Quigley
Duane E. Smith
Jane G. Sure

General Editor
Judith A. Matz

Production Directors
Kerin Martin
Theresa Richard
Evelyn C. Davis

Staff Associates
Arlene Chatman
Michael Leong
Alita Letwin
Louis E. Rosen
Howard Safier

Consulting Associates
Gloria Eastman
Leslie Hendrikson
Barbara Miller
Eugenia Moore
David Morgan
Laurel Singleton
John Zola

Art Director and Illustrator
Richard Stein

Typesetters
Roslyn Danberg
Jan Ruyle

Production Assistant
Lise Borja

The Center is also grateful for the many helpful comments and suggestions that have been received from the following persons who have reviewed the manuscript in its various developmental stages. The Center has attempted to be responsive to all of the many valuable suggestions for improvement in the text. However, the final product is the responsibility of the Center and does not necessarily reflect the views of those who have contributed their thoughts and ideas.

A. L. Block
Director of Instruction
Franklin School District
Franklin, Wisconsin

Margaret Branson
Administrator
Division of Instructional Services
Kern County Public Schools
Kern Country, California

Gary Bryner
Professor
Department of Political Science
Brigham Young University
Provo, Utah

Libby Cupp
Coordinator
Consumer Affairs
Apollo Career Center
Lima, Ohio

Lorenca Rosal Douglas
Executive Director
New Hampshire Law Related
Education
Concord, New Hampshire

Tami Dowler
Area Director for UniServ
Kentucky Education
Association
Frankfort, Kentucky

Michael Fischer
Associate
Bureau of Social Studies
New York State Education
Department
Albany, New York

James R. Giese
Executive Director
Social Science Education
Consortium, Inc.
Boulder, Colorado

Jeanne Kress
Teacher
Country Dale Elementary School
Franklin, Wisconsin

Joan Parrish
Demonstration Teacher
Corinne A. Seeds University
Elementary School
Westwood, California

Dorothy Skeel
Director
Peabody Center for Economic
and Social Studies
George Peabody College of
Vanderbilt University
Nashville, Tennessee

Connie Yeaton
Coordinator
Indiana State Law Related
Education Project of the
Indiana Bar Association
Columbus, Ohio

Warren E. Burger, Chairman

Commission on the Bicentennial of the United States Constitution

Chief Justice of the United States, 1969-1986

The years 1987 to 1991 mark the 200th anniversary of the writing, ratification, and implementation of the basic documents of American democracy, the Constitution and the Bill of Rights. Our Constitution has stood the tests and stresses of time, wars and change. Although it was not perfect, as Benjamin Franklin and many others recognized, it has lasted because it was carefully crafted by men who understood the importance of a system of government sufficiently strong to meet the challenges of the day, yet sufficiently flexible to accommodate and adapt to new political, economic, and social conditions.

Many Americans have but a slight understanding of the Constitution, the Bill of Rights, and the later amendments to which we pledge our allegiance. The lessons in this book are designed to give you, the next generation of American citizens, an understanding of the background, creation, and subsequent history of the unique system of government brought into being by our Constitution. At the same time, it will help you understand the principles and ideals that underlie and give meaning to the Constitution, a system of government by those governed.

Table of Contents

Introduction

You have the right to hold any religious beliefs you wish to hold. You also have the right not to hold any religious beliefs at all.

If you are arrested for a crime, you have a right to have a lawyer help defend you.

When you become 18 years old, you have the right to vote in all elections.

Members of the Senate must run for election every six years.

The President of the United States cannot stop an election from being held.

All these things are true in the United States. They might not be true in other countries. Why are they true here?

These things are true in our country because they are written in our **Constitution**. Our Constitution is a **written plan** that says what our government should do. It also says how our government is to be organized and run.

The most important thing the Constitution does is **limit the powers** of government. The Constitution describes what members of our government may do. It also says what they may **not** do. The Constitution helps prevent the government from violating our rights.

Our Constitution is the highest or **supreme law** of our land. Even the President, Congress, and the Supreme Court must obey the Constitution. In our country, everyone must obey the law.

Our Constitution was written and adopted in Philadelphia 200 years ago. We need to understand our Constitution to know our rights and responsibilities as citizens.

This book is not like most history books. Most history books tell the story of people and events of the past. This book is a **history of ideas**. It explains the most important ideas of our Constitution and tells you how they were developed.

This book will help you understand some of the basic ideals, or goals, of our nation. These ideals include the belief in liberty and justice for all people. You also will learn about your responsibilities as a citizen to help make these ideals a reality for everyone.

The title of each lesson in this book asks an important question about government. After you have finished the lesson, you should be able to answer the question. The answers to these questions will help you understand why the Constitution is important for you.

Reviewing important ideas

1. What is our Constitution?
2. What is the most important thing our Constitution does?

Class projects

As you study each unit in this text, think about the most important things you have learned. Your class might want to create a bulletin board display. It could include the following things.

- Pictures, stories, or articles that show the most important ideas you have studied in each unit.

- A timeline of important events related to our history. In each unit, you will discover new events to add to your timeline.

- A map of the thirteen original colonies that shows important events in our history. In each unit, you will find some ideas to illustrate your map.

Unit One

What were the Founders' basic ideas about government?

What ideas did the Founders have about good government?

Our Constitution was written by fifty-five men who met in Philadelphia in 1787. In four months they wrote a constitution which has lasted over 200 years!

To understand our Constitution, you need to know something about the knowledge and experiences of the men who wrote it. You also need to know something about their ideas about government.

In this unit, we will look at what people in America were like in the 1770s. We also will learn about their history and their basic ideas about government. Finally, we will learn how Americans created their first national government.

LESSON 1

What was America like in the 1770s?

If you lived in America in 1770, what would your life be like?

Purpose of Lesson

In the 1700s, there were British, French, and Spanish colonies in North America. In this book, we will look at the British colonies because they became the United States of America. They became our original thirteen states.

To understand the people who wrote our Constitution, you should know something about what their lives were like. In this lesson, you will learn how most Americans lived 200 years ago.

4

Our country first belonged to Great Britain

There was no United States of America in the early 1770s. We had no constitution, no states, no national government. There were no highways, television, or automobiles. It was a very different country. If you went back in time, you would hardly recognize the America that you live in now.

In the early 1770s, Americans lived in thirteen **colonies** along the Atlantic coast. We were not independent then. During our early history, Great Britain ruled the American colonies. Great Britain was a powerful country more than two thousand miles away across the Atlantic Ocean. Let's find out more about what America was like in the 1770s.

colonies
settlements ruled by another country

Turn back the clock

Get into your time machine and turn the dial to 1775. Take a trip back in time. You are now living in one of the thirteen British colonies in North America. You are a citizen of Great Britain and a subject of His Majesty, George III.

It is an exciting time but you are a little nervous. You have heard your parents talk about how the British are trying to take away the rights of the colonists. Some people even talk of a war. You and your friends argue about who is right — the colonists or the British. You debate what kind of government Americans should have.

Think about America in 1775. What was it like? How would you describe America? What makes it special to you? This lesson will help you answer these questions.

5

What was America like 200 years ago?

One of the first things visitors to America noticed was the huge size of this country. It was a very large place compared to most nations in Europe. In the 1770s, there was a great deal of open, unsettled space. Settlers living in the British colonies were scattered along the eastern coast from Maine to Georgia.

MAINE (part of MASS.)

N.H.

NEW YORK

MASS. • Boston

• Plymouth

CONN. R.I. • Providence

PENNSYLVANIA

• New York

NEW JERSEY

• Philadelphia

APPALACHIAN MOUNTAINS

MARYLAND

DELAWARE

VIRGINIA

ATLANTIC OCEAN

• Williamsburg

NORTH CAROLINA

SOUTH CAROLINA

GEORGIA • Charleston

THE THIRTEEN COLONIES

There was room in America for people to settle and to own land. The opportunity to buy land attracted many new **immigrants**. In Europe, only the rich could afford to buy land. In the colonies, it was different. Land was cheap and immigrants came with the hope of owning their own land. Owning land meant not only that you could support your family, but also that you could vote.

No matter how quickly the population grew, there seemed to be plenty of land. In 1775, there were 2.5 million people in America. Fifteen years later, there were almost 4 million people. The population continued to grow quickly. However, it took more than a hundred years before people settled in all parts of what is now the United States.

Who were the Americans?

Many Americans, or their families, had originally come from Great Britain. As a result, they spoke English and had many British ways. They dressed like the British. They practiced the Protestant religion and followed many of the British customs. However, the American colonists were also different in some ways from the British.

In Great Britain, most people had the same background, race, and language. But that was not true in the colonies. People from many different lands came to live in America. Each group of settlers brought with them their own customs and ways of life. Settlers came from many different countries in Europe—from Germany, France, Sweden, Spain, and the Netherlands. No wonder visitors to our country spoke about the **diversity** of the colonists.

Many Native Americans also lived in the colonies. They had lived here for a long time before the thirteen colonies were settled. By the 1770s, however, the colonists had pushed some tribes off the land they lived on. These tribes had moved further west.

There were about 500,000 black people who had originally been brought from Africa. This was 20% or one-fifth of the population of the entire country. Most of these black people lived as **slaves** in the Southern colonies.

The diversity among Americans helped create a society that was special. From our early years, America was a home for many different people.

How did Americans live?

Most Americans in the 1770s were farmers, but not all farms were alike. It depended on where you lived. In the Northern colonies the cold climate made farming more difficult. A farm might be only a small fifty-acre patch of rocky soil. On such a farm, the family would do all the work themselves. Sometimes they would hire a person to help them. They might have an **indentured servant**.

In the South, the warmer climate made farming easier. Most of the people lived on small farms much like the people in New England. Some people lived on large farms called **plantations**. Most of these plantations had some slaves to help with the work. A few families lived on plantations with thousands of acres. These plantations often had hundreds of slaves.

Americans were much more **self-sufficient** than people are today. They raised their own food and wove their own cloth for clothes. They built homes and barns, made their own furniture and tools, and even made their own medicines. They traded any extra farm products at local stores for those few goods they could not make for themselves.

slave
a person who is owned as property

indentured servant
a person who agreed to work for a certain period of time in exchange for the cost of coming to America

self-sufficient
able to provide most of one's own needs

How do you think life on a Northern farm might
have been different from life on a Southern plantation?

Opportunities in America

A newcomer to America would have been impressed by how well the colonists lived. Americans of the 1770s lived better than most people anywhere else in the world. They worked hard, but the land was fertile and they grew plenty of food. Most Americans ate better and were taller and healthier than people in Europe.

Americans also were better educated than most Europeans. More people in America could read and write than in any other nation in the world. Many colonists owned enough property to be able to vote. There were opportunities to become wealthy or to be elected to a government position.

Which of these people do you think could vote in the 1770s?

Not all people, however, had the same opportunities. Usually the colonies only permitted adult white men who owned property to vote. Women, blacks, Native Americans, and white men who did not own property usually were not allowed to vote. They could not be elected to the government. Most women were not allowed to own property. Slaves had no rights.

Even with these limits, most Americans still had more rights and opportunities than did people in Europe. These rights and opportunities were very important to them. By 1775, the colonists were worried about how to protect their rights.

What opportunities did Americans have in the 1770s?

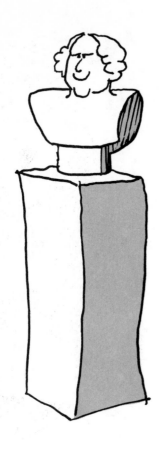

Do you think the colonists liked being ruled by King George III?

Who governed the colonies?

Great Britain ruled the American colonies from 1607 to 1776, more than 150 years. During much of this time, Great Britain was busy with problems in Europe. The British government did not pay much attention to the colonies. Leaders in the American colonies learned to govern themselves. They had brought British customs and laws with them to America. They used these British ideas to develop their own governments. The colonists participated in their governments much more than people did in Europe.

During the 1770s, Americans thought about what kind of government they wanted. They asked themselves whether Great Britain was really protecting their rights. There were many arguments, speeches, and books about what was best for the colonies. If you had lived in America then, you would have found it an exciting time.

Who were the Founders?

There were many important leaders in early America. For example, George Washington, Patrick Henry, Abigail Adams, and Benjamin Franklin were all well-known during this time. You probably have heard of some of these people. We call these leaders the **Founders** because they helped found, or establish, our country.

Why were the Founders important?

The Founders led the fight to free our country from British rule. They developed their own ideas about what type of government would be best for America. The next lessons will help you understand the ideas the Founders used to create our government.

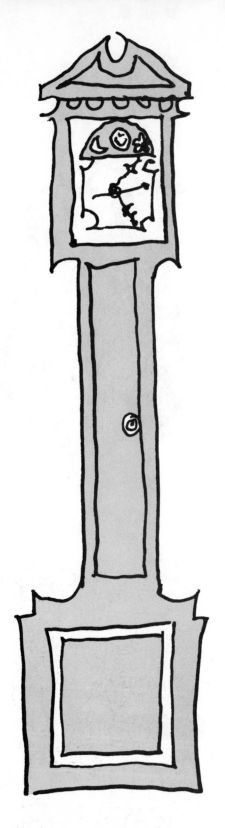

Reviewing and using the lesson

1. Describe the life of an average American of the 1770s.

2. Do you think the average American had a good life? Why or why not? Would you have wanted to live in America in the 1770s?

3. Why do you think many Europeans wanted to live in America in 1770?

4. Do you think the way Americans lived might have influenced their ideas about government? Explain your answer.

5. How do you think a slave would describe his or her life in America?

6. Look at a map of the United States today. Find the original thirteen colonies. What were the names of the thirteen colonies? Which was the most northern colony? Which was the most southern colony? Which of the thirteen colonies bordered the Atlantic Ocean?

7. Locate your state. Was your state originally a British colony? Was it a French or Spanish colony? When did your state become part of the United States?

8. Explain these terms: colony, immigrant, diversity, slave, indentured servant, plantation, self-sufficient, Founders.

Why did the Founders think we needed a government?

Purpose of Lesson

In this lesson you will learn some of the Founders' most important ideas about government. You will learn about your rights and where they come from. Finally, you will learn why the Founders believed we needed a government.

When you finish this lesson, you should be able to explain the Founders' ideas about our rights and the purposes of our government.

Problem solving

What are your beliefs about rights?

Before learning about the Founders' beliefs about rights, let's examine your ideas about rights. Then you can compare your ideas with theirs. You will probably find that you and the Founders have many of the same ideas.

Do you think you should have the right to believe in any religion you wish? Do you think you should have a right to be protected from people who try to break into your home and steal your property? You probably agree that you should have these and other rights.

Work together in groups of about three to five students to answer the questions on the next page.

What rights do you think you have?

15

1. What are rights?

2. List the rights you think you should have. Why do you think it is important for you to have these rights?

3. Which rights, if any, seem most important? Why?

What were the Founders' beliefs about rights?

Most of the Founders believed that you and everyone else have certain **basic rights**. These are the rights to **life**, **liberty**, and **property**. The following are examples of what these rights mean.

- **Life.** The right to live without the fear of being injured or killed by others.

- **Liberty.** The right to be free. The right to believe what you wish, to read what you want, to speak freely, and to travel freely wherever you want to go.

- **Property.** The right to own such things as clothes, books, toys, bicycles, cars, homes, businesses, and factories.

The Founders called these rights their **natural rights.** Some Founders believed that we get these rights from God. Others believed that we have them just because it is natural for people to have them. It is natural to breathe, to eat, and to sleep. It is also natural to be free to live as you want. It is natural to believe and speak as you wish.

natural rights
the right to life, liberty, and property

Why do we need to protect our rights?

The Founders agreed that we all have the right to life, liberty, and property. They worried about how those rights could be protected.

The Founders knew that sometimes people try to take other people's rights away from them. They thought about the best ways to protect their rights. To do this, they imagined what life might be like without rules, laws, or government.

How can we protect our rights?

Could you play baseball without rules?

Problem solving

What do you think might happen if there were no rules, laws, or government?

Imagine what might happen if we had no rules or laws. What if we did not have any government? To understand what might happen without laws or government, imagine trying to play baseball with no rules and no umpire. Suppose there were no rules about driving or no laws saying children had to go to school.

Work together in groups of about three to five students. Answer the following questions and be prepared to present your answers to the class.

1. What might happen in a country if there were no rules or laws?

2. What might happen if there were rules and laws, but no one to make sure people obeyed them?

3. What might happen if there were rules and laws, but no one to settle disagreements about them?

What did the Founders think might happen without rules, laws, and government?

You probably have thought of some of the same answers the Founders did. The Founders thought that life would be extremely difficult without laws or government. They thought these problems might happen:

1. Some people might try to take away other people's rights.

    - Stronger people might force weaker people to do what they wanted them to do.

    - Weaker people might join together and take away the rights of the stronger people.

2. No one would feel safe.

The Founders believed that nobody's rights would really be protected without laws and government. They believed it would be very hard to live a safe, peaceful, and happy life under these conditions.

How does the government protect our rights?

What is the purpose of government?

consent
to agree

The Founders thought the best way to protect our rights was for people to **consent** to form a government and to obey its laws. The main **purpose** of such a government would be to **protect people's rights** to life, liberty, and property.

The Founders learned these ideas from their study of history and government. Some of their ideas also came from their religious beliefs. You will learn more about the Founders' ideas in the next lesson.

Many of the Founders studied the ideas of John Locke. He was a writer who lived in England in the 17th century. The Founders used his ideas in planning our government.

Reviewing and using the lesson

1. What basic rights do you think people should have?

2. How can people's rights be protected?

3. What did the Founders think should be the main purpose of our government? Do you agree? Explain your position.

4. Draw a cartoon that illustrates your own definition of the word "government" and share it with your classmates.

5. Explain these terms: natural rights, consent.

What is a republican government?

Purpose of Lesson

This lesson will help you understand why the Founders thought a republican form of government was best. You will also learn about civic virtue and the common welfare.

The Founders studied history

The Founders studied the history of governments. They were very interested in what they read about the government of the Roman Republic. It was located in what is now the country of Italy. The Roman Republic existed more than 2,000 years before our nation began.

The Founders liked what they read about the Roman Republic. They learned some important ideas from their study of the government of ancient Rome. They used some of these ideas when they created our government.

What is a republican government?

The government of Rome was called a **republican government**. The Founders read that republican government was one in which:

- The **power** of government is held by the people.

- The **people** give power to leaders they **elect** to **represent** them and serve their **interests**.

- The **representatives** are responsible for helping all the people in the country, not just a few people.

interests
those things which are to a person's benefit

representatives
people elected to act for others

Why would elections be an important part of a republican government?

What are the advantages of republican government?

The Founders thought a republican government was the best kind of government they could choose for themselves. They believed that the advantages of republican government were:

- **Fairness.** They believed that laws made by the representatives they elected would be fair. If their representatives did not make fair laws, they could elect others who would.

- **Common welfare.** The laws would help everyone instead of one person or a few favored people.

- **Freedom and prosperity.** People would have greater freedom and be able to live well.

What is the common welfare?

When a government tries to help everyone in a country, we say it is serving the **common welfare**. The common welfare is what is good for everyone in the country, not just a few people.

Is this government serving the common welfare?

Problem solving

Your interests and the common welfare

How do you decide what the common welfare is? When should you give up your own interests to do something that is good for everyone? Each person has to answer this question for himself or herself. The following exercise will help you do this.

Work in groups of about three to five students. Each group should discuss the following questions. Be prepared to explain your group's answers to the class.

1. Describe a situation in which you think you should try to help others instead of just doing what you want for yourself.

2. Explain a situation in which you think you should do something for yourself instead of trying to help others.

3. Sometimes people disagree about what is the best thing for everyone. Describe a situation where this might happen. How do you think such disagreements should be settled?

4. Describe some things your government does to help everyone in the country. What other things could your government do? Why?

When should you put the needs of others above your own interests?

What is civic virtue?

When you work to help others and promote the common welfare, you are showing **civic virtue**. The Founders thought civic virtue was important for a republican government. People with civic virtue are interested in having the government help all the people.

The Founders thought it was necessary to teach children the importance of helping others. Young people learned about civic virtue in their homes, schools, and churches. Adults also heard about civic virtue from their religious and political leaders.

The Founders thought a republican government would work in our country. They believed most of the people had civic virtue. They thought the people would select leaders who would work for the common welfare.

How did the colonists learn about civic virtue?

Reviewing and using the lesson

1. What is republican government?

2. Define "common welfare." Give examples of how your school helps the common welfare.

3. Define "civic virtue." Give examples of people with civic virtue in your school and community.

4. Where was civic virtue taught in early America?

5. Describe a situation in which your interests might conflict with the common welfare.

6. Explain these terms: republican government, representative, interests, common welfare, civic virtue.

LESSON 4

What is a constitutional government?

Purpose of Lesson

You have learned some of the main ideas the Founders used when they created our government. Two other important ideas are included in this lesson: (1) the idea of a constitution, and (2) the idea of a constitutional government.

When you have finished this lesson, you should be able to explain these two ideas.

Problem solving

Complete the following exercise in groups of three to five students. Be prepared to explain your findings to the class.

Read the list of rules and laws on the next page. For each rule or law, follow these instructions.

- Write the number of each rule or law that tells something about how a government is to be run. Be prepared to explain what the rule or law says about how a government is to be run.

- Then, write the number of each rule or law that does **not** tell something about how a government is to be run.

1. Congress cannot make any laws that unfairly limit your right to speak freely.

2. Don't speak with your mouth full.

3. Take turns on the swings on the playground.

4. The king can choose the people he wants to be judges and generals.

5. You must finish your assignment before you go out for recess.

6. The President must be elected every four years.

7. A person must be sixteen to get a driver's license.

What is a constitution?

In the above exercise, you should have found some rules and laws that tell how a government is to be run. You also should have found some rules that do not say anything about how a government is to be run.

When you found the rules and laws that tell how a government is to be run, you found parts of a **constitution**. A constitution is a set of rules and laws that tells how a government is organized and run. Most constitutions are written. Some are partly unwritten. Some are not written at all.

Studying the constitution of a government will help you answer certain questions about that government and its citizens. Here are some of the questions a constitution usually answers.

Questions about the government

- What are the purposes of the government?

- How is the government organized? For example, what parts does it have? What does each part do?

- How is the government supposed to go about doing its business? For example, how are rules made?

- How are people chosen to serve in the government?

Questions about citizens

- Who is considered to be a citizen?

- Are citizens supposed to have control over their government? If so, how do they control it?

- What rights and responsibilities, if any, are the citizens supposed to have?

According to our definition, every nation has a constitution. Fair governments and unfair governments have constitutions.

What is a constitutional government?

limited
restricted

Having a constitution does **not** mean that a nation has a constitutional government. A nation has a **constitutional government** when the powers of the person or group running the government are **limited**. For example, our Constitution limits the powers of the President. The President cannot do something just because he or she wants to.

It is not enough just to describe the limits on the powers of government. In a constitutional government, the people running the government must obey the constitution. The constitution contains ways to make sure the people in the government obey the limits on their power.

How do you think the right to a trial by jury limits the power of the government?

What is a dictatorial government?

A **dictator** is a person running a government who has **unlimited power** to do whatever he or she wants. How can you have a dictatorial government if you have a constitution?

- The constitution itself may give the dictator unlimited power.

- The constitution may say that the government's power is limited without providing ways to enforce those limits.

- The limits that are in the constitution may not actually be enforced.

In a dictatorial government, power is unlimited. That is why dictatorial governments are not called constitutional governments, even though they have constitutions.

What can happen when a ruler has unlimited power?

Problem solving

Why is it important to limit a government's powers?

You have learned that constitutional governments have limits on their powers. Why do we need such limits? The following story may help you understand why. It is based on part of a book called *Two Years Before the Mast*. This book was written by a famous American author, Richard Henry Dana (1815-1882). The book is a true story of Dana's experiences. When he was young, he worked on a ship that sailed from New England around South America to the West Coast.

At that time, there were no laws that placed reasonable limits on the power of a ship's captain. Because of this story and the efforts of other people, laws were passed to limit the powers of ship captains.

When you have finished reading, answer the questions at the end of the story.

Life on a sailing ship

The captain of our ship had been losing his temper about a lot of things. He threatened to whip the cook for throwing wood on the deck. He got furious when the mate bragged that he could tie knots better than the captain. However, most of his anger was directed against Sam.

Sam couldn't speak very well and he worked more slowly than most. But he was a pretty good sailor and he tried to do his best. The captain just didn't like him.

One Saturday morning, I heard the captain shouting at someone. Then I heard the noises of a fight.

"You may as well keep still, for I have got you," said the captain. "Will you ever talk back to me again?"

"I never did, sir," said Sam.

"That's not what I asked you. Will you ever talk back to me again?"

"I never have," Sam said again.

"Answer my question, or I'll have you whipped!"

"I'm no slave," said Sam.

"Then I'll make you one," said the captain. He sprang up to the deck and called the mate. "Tie that man up! I'll teach you all who is master of this ship!"

"What are you going to whip that man for, sir?" said John, the Swede, to the captain.

Upon hearing this, the captain turned to John and ordered him to be put in chains.

Watching this made me sick. I wanted to stop it. But there were only a few others who felt like me. If we started a fight, we would lose. Then we would be accused of mutiny. Even if we won, we would have to be pirates for life. If we were ever caught, we would be punished. A sailor has no rights. He has to do what the captain orders or become a pirate.

The captain whipped both men without mercy. When John asked why he was being whipped, the captain answered, "Because you ask questions." Then he whipped him harder and harder.

I was horrified. I couldn't watch any more.

At last the captain stopped. He turned to us. "Now you see how things are! Now you know what I am! I'm the slave driver, and you are all my slaves! I'll make you all do as I say or I'll whip you all!"

Answer the following questions about the story you have just read. Be prepared to share your answers with the class.

1. Were there any limits on the power of the ship's captain? Explain your answer.

2. Were there any ways to protect the rights of the sailors? Explain your answer.

3. Was the government of the ship like a constitutional government? Why or why not?

4. Was the government of the ship like a dictatorial government? Why or why not?

5. What laws would you suggest should be made to protect the rights of the sailors? Explain your answer.

Reviewing and using the lesson

1. What can you learn about a nation's government by studying its constitution?

2. Explain the differences between constitutional governments and dictatorial governments.

3. Role play a board of inquiry formed to look into the event described in the story. A group of about five students should serve as the board. Other students should take the parts of persons in the story. The board should conduct a hearing to determine what happened. Then the board should suggest new laws to prevent this kind of situation from happening again.

4. Explain these terms: constitution, limits, constitutional government, dictatorial government.

LESSON 5

How did the Founders use their ideas in the Declaration of Independence?

Purpose of Lesson

In 1776 the American colonies decided to break away from British rule. They chose to be a free country. The Founders wrote a special statement to explain why they wanted to be independent. This statement is called the **Declaration of Independence**.

The Declaration of Independence is one of the most important writings in American history. It describes the major ideas the Founders had about government. The Declaration also contains the Founders' complaints against the British king.

When you have finished this lesson, you should be able to explain some of the main ideas in the Declaration. As you will see, they are ideas you have already studied and discussed.

Why did the Founders want independence?

For many years, the British government let the colonists govern themselves with little interference. Britain was often busy fighting wars with other European countries. But in the 1760s, Britain began to tighten its control over the colonies. The British government passed new laws taxing the colonists and controlling their trade. Many colonists thought these laws threatened their right to govern themselves.

NEW WORLD   colonies

Great Britain

OLD WORLD

France

The colonists became alarmed because they felt their rights were not being protected. The colonists did not have the right to vote for people to represent them in the British government. Some Americans argued that the British government had no right to tax them. They said, "No taxation without representation!"

Look at the two pictures on this page. What do they tell you about the change in Britain's attitude toward the colonies?

Colonies

Great Britain

Great Britain felt it had the right to tax the colonies and control their trade. People in Britain were paying high taxes to support and defend the American colonies. They thought the Americans should have to pay their share of the taxes. If the colonists received the benefits of being part of Great Britain, they should pay for them.

Many Americans became angry about the new trade laws and taxes passed by the British government. In 1774, the colonists sent representatives to a meeting called the **First Continental Congress** to decide what to do. Some people suggested stopping trade with Britain. They thought this action might make the British government change its laws. Other colonists did not agree. Soon there was talk of fighting the British.

In April, 1775, war broke out between Britain and the American colonies. The **American Revolution** had begun. The thirteen colonies became the thirteen original **states** of our country.

First Continental Congress

meeting of colonial representatives in 1774 called to protest British laws

Why did the colonists write the Declaration of Independence?

Why was the Declaration of Independence written?

Soon after the war began, the American colonists created a new government for themselves. In 1776, the new government formed a committee to tell everyone why the colonists wanted to free themselves from British rule.

Thomas Jefferson was chosen to head this committee. He was not a very good public speaker but was considered an excellent writer. The paper he wrote became known as the **Declaration of Independence**. It contains the basic ideals of the new nation. On July 4, 1776, the Declaration was signed by the members of the Continental Congress.

What does the Declaration of Independence say?

The Declaration of Independence was important in the development of our government. The Founders used some of the main ideas you have studied to explain why they wanted to be a free nation. The Declaration of Independence contains the

- **ideals** or goals of our nation.
- **complaints** of the colonists against the British king.
- **arguments** the colonists used to explain why they were freeing themselves from British rule.

The Declaration ends by saying that the colonies should be free and independent states. These parts of the Declaration are so important it is worth learning more about them.

Ideals of the Declaration

The Declaration tells some of the **ideals** of our government. Ideals are something perfect that we try to achieve.

For example, one of the ideals in the Declaration is that all people are created equal. Because of this, all people have certain basic rights. These are the rights to life, liberty, and the chance to seek happiness.

Complaints of the Declaration

When you read the Declaration, you will find a long list of complaints against King George III. The Founders wanted to tell everyone how the King and the British government had threatened their rights. They wanted to defend their revolt against Great Britain. Here is a list of some of the Founders' complaints against the King. They complained that the King had

- refused to approve laws made by the colonists.
- kept armies in the colonies when there was no war.
- stopped the colonists' trade with other countries.
- taxed the colonists without their consent.
- taken away the colonists' right to a trial by jury.

Arguments of the Declaration

The Declaration explains why the Founders thought they had the right to free themselves from British rule. Here are three of the most important reasons.

- **Government is based upon consent.** The Founders argued that the colonists had an agreement with the King. They had **consented** to be governed by him only as long as he protected their natural rights.

- **The right to change the government.** The Founders said that if a government takes away people's natural rights, the people can change or do away with the government and form a new one.

- **The King had broken the agreement.** The Founders said the King had tried to take away the people's rights. He had broken his agreement with the colonists. Therefore, they did not have to continue to be governed by him. They were free to set up their own government.

Why did the colonists want to be free of British rule?

Problem solving

Which side would you support?

It was difficult for many Americans to decide which side to support during the Revolution. Those who supported the Revolution were known as **Patriots**. Those who wanted to continue to be loyal to the British king were known as **Loyalists**.

It is important to understand the differences between the Patriots and the Loyalists. To help you do this, your class should be divided into small groups or two large groups. Half of the groups should take the Patriot position and the other half should represent the Loyalists. After each group has presented its position, the class should decide which side—Patriot or Loyalist—has the stronger argument.

- Patriots: Write a letter to a newspaper or draw a picture defending the position of the colonists who wanted to free themselves from British rule.

- Loyalists: Write a letter to a newspaper or draw a picture defending the Loyalists' position. Explain why you think the colonists should remain part of Great Britain.

Do you think you would have been a Loyalist in 1776?

Reviewing and using the lesson

1. What was the purpose of the Declaration of Independence?

2. Where does the Declaration say that governments get their power?

3. What does the Declaration say people have a right to do if government does not protect their rights?

4. What do you think is meant by the phrase "all men are created equal"?

5. What are the most important ideals of the Declaration of Independence? Why are they important to you?

6. Part of the Declaration of Independence is printed below. Some of the words may be new to you. The meanings of these words are given in brackets after the words. Rewrite the Declaration in your own words. Be prepared to explain the ideas in this part of the Declaration.

> We hold these Truths to be self-evident [easy for anyone to see],
>
> that all Men are created equal,
>
> that they are endowed [given] by their Creator [God] with certain unalienable Rights [basic or natural rights that cannot be taken away],
>
> that among these are Life, Liberty, and the Pursuit of Happiness —
>
> That to secure these Rights, Governments are instituted [set up] among Men, deriving [getting] their just Powers from the Consent [agreement] of the Governed,
>
> that whenever any Form of Government becomes destructive of these Ends [purposes], it is the Right of the People to alter [change] or to abolish [get rid of] it, and to institute new Government....

7. Explain these terms: Declaration of Independence, First Continental Congress, American Revolution, ideals.

LESSON 6

What was our first national government like?

Purpose of Lesson

After the Declaration of Independence was signed, the Founders needed to create a government for the new nation. Our first constitution was called the Articles of Confederation. It was approved in 1781.

When you have completed this lesson, you should be able to describe the government under the Articles of Confederation. You should also be able to explain how the problems caused by this government led the Founders to write a new constitution.

What kind of government should we create?

Get back into your time machine. Set the dial for 1776. You are no longer a subject of Great Britain. The Declaration of Independence has been signed. You are now a citizen of a new nation—the United States of America.

The American colonies are free and independent states. Each has its own state government. But who will govern the country? Who will lead the war against Great Britain? There is no **national government**.

You are now a member of the Continental Congress. You have been appointed to the committee that is writing our first constitution. It is a difficult task. Each state has its own interests. How can you write a constitution that will satisfy all the states? What kind of national government should you create?

YEAR
1776
MONTH
AUGUST

national government
organization governing an entire country

42

There were two main problems the Founders faced when they tried to create a national government:

What problems did the Founders face when they created our first national government?

1. The fear of a national government with too much power. Many of the Founders feared a strong government might take away the rights of the states and the people.

2. The fear that some states would have more power than others in the new government.

Both these fears influenced the Founders when they created our first national government. As a result, they chose to set up a **weak** national government with very limited powers.

43

legislature
*the part of a government
that makes the laws*

The most important part of the new government was the **legislature.** It was called **Congress.** The powers of Congress were very limited. The states made sure they kept most of the power for themselves. Each state — no matter how big or small or how many people it had — had one vote in Congress. The national government could not do anything important without having the approval of the state governments.

After much debate and disagreement, the Articles of Confederation were approved by the states in 1781. This was our constitution for seven years. Let's look at the achievements and problems of the Articles.

Achievements under the Articles of Confederation

The Articles of Confederation created a government that helped keep our country together during the Revolution. During this time, the national government was responsible for a number of important achievements.

- The United States won the war for independence against Great Britain.

- The government made a peace **treaty** with Great Britain to end the American Revolution.

- Each state had to respect the laws of the other states. For example, if you were married in one state, the other states also would consider you married. You could travel freely from one state to another without needing a passport.

- Congress passed the **Northwest Ordinance** of 1787. This law allowed people in the western territories to organize their own governments. When they were ready, they could ask to become new states. The law provided for public education in these areas. It also said slavery would not be permitted in any new states made from this territory.

What were important accomplishments of our government under the Articles of Confederation?

Problems under the Articles of Confederation

The government also had many problems under the Articles of Confederation. Some of the most important are described on the next page.

● When the Revolution was over, each state began to act like a separate country. Each had its own interests. People did not think of themselves as citizens of the United States. They thought of themselves as citizens of their own states. They were Virginians, New Yorkers, or South Carolinians—for example—but not Americans. Many times the state governments would not cooperate to solve their problems.

What do you think happened when the states refused to cooperate?

- By 1786, many Americans were having a difficult time making a living. Businesses were failing. Trade between states and with different nations was not good. Many people owed money to others. Soldiers who had fought in the Revolution still had not been paid.

What do you think happened when Congress asked the states for money?

- The national government under the Articles of Confederation was too weak. It did not have the power to unite the country. It had no money and no power to get it. It could not control the states. It could not help solve problems between the states.

Shays' Rebellion

Within the states, there were also problems. For example, in Massachusetts many farmers had no money. When they could not pay their bills, they lost their farms and homes. Some were even put in prison for not being able to pay their bills. Many people felt this was unfair and protested.

What were Shays and his followers trying to do?

In November 1786, several hundred angry farmers gathered under the leadership of Daniel Shays. They were ready to fight against the Massachusetts government. They tried to capture weapons to use in their struggle.

State troops finally stopped **Shays' Rebellion** but it frightened many property owners. People worried that such rebellions could spread to other states. Who would protect their property?

How should we improve our national government?

The Founders decided there were too many problems with the national government under the Articles of Confederation. It was time to improve it. Congress agreed. It called for a meeting to be held in Philadelphia in 1787. Each state was asked to send representatives to this meeting.

The meeting in Philadelphia was supposed to suggest ways to improve the Articles of Confederation. However, once the delegates met, they decided that the Articles had too many problems. They put the Articles aside and wrote a new constitution.

Reviewing and using the lesson

1. Why did the Founders create a weak national government?

2. If we did not have a national government, each state would be a separate country. Each state might have its own army, its own money, and its own trade rules. What problems might happen in this situation?

3. What were some of the achievements of the national government under the Articles of Confederation?

4. What were some of the problems that happened under the Articles of Confederation?

5. Describe Shays' Rebellion. Why was it important?

6. Explain these terms: Articles of Confederation, national government, treaty, Congress, Northwest Ordinance, Shays' Rebellion.

Unit Two

How was our Constitution written?

How did the Framers write our Constitution?

This unit will describe how the **Framers** wrote the Constitution at a convention in Philadelphia. Fifty-five men attended the Philadelphia Convention. They were the Framers of our Constitution.

The convention lasted from May to September 1787. The Framers worked together for four months to write our Constitution. It has lasted over 200 years!

Suppose you and the other members of your class were the Framers. You are meeting in Philadelphia to write a new constitution. You share the same basic ideas about government. You all believe your government should protect your rights and promote the common welfare. You believe you should have the right to elect representatives to protect your interests. You also think there should be clear limits on the powers of the national government.

As Framers, you have read about the history of government. You have had experiences with the governments of your states. These experiences make you understand it is important to plan a government carefully. You know that if you don't write a good constitution, your government might take away your rights.

Sharing much of the same knowledge, experiences, and beliefs might help you agree on how to write a constitution. Yet there are also differences among you. Different members of your class have different backgrounds, beliefs, and ideas.

In the same way, there were differences among the Framers in Philadelphia. Some were from states with large populations and some from small states. Some were from the North, which had few slaves, and some from the South, where there were many slaves. These differences led to disagreements about what should be in the Constitution.

This unit will help you understand why the Framers wrote our Constitution the way they did. It will tell you of some of the agreements and disagreements among the Framers. You will learn how the Framers made compromises to solve their disagreements.

When you have completed the unit, you should be able to explain how the Constitution was written.

LESSON 7

How did the Philadelphia Convention begin?

Purpose of Lesson

In the last lesson you learned that the Philadelphia Convention was called to correct some of the problems of the Articles of Confederation. In this lesson you will learn who some of the important Framers were. You will also learn about some of the decisions they made at the beginning of the convention.

Problem solving

Who should participate in creating a government?

Suppose your principal decided to give a group of students the task of creating a constitution for your student government. Meet in groups of about five students each and answer the following questions. Be prepared to report your answers to the class.

1. Should each class in your school have the right to send representatives to the meeting? Why or why not?

2. Should some classes be able to send more representatives than others? Why or why not?

3. How many votes should each class have? Why?

4. How should class representatives be selected? Why?

5. What qualifications should representatives have? Why?

6. What responsibilities should representatives have? Why?

7. Which of the basic ideas about government that you have studied did you use in answering these questions?

Who were the Framers?

Fifty-five **delegates** attended the Philadelphia Convention. All were white men. Their average age was forty-two. That may seem old to you, but they were young for such an important task. Many of these men had been leaders during the American Revolution. About three-fourths of them had served in Congress. Most were leaders in their states. Some were rich, but most were not. None were poor.

delegates
people chosen to represent others at a meeting

The delegates were not chosen from all parts of the American population. There were no women among the delegates. There were no Native Americans. There were no free black men or slaves. Poor farmers—like those who took part in Shays' Rebellion—were not present either. Nor were the citizens of Rhode Island. People in Rhode Island were so much against changing the Articles of Confederation that they refused to send any delegates!

Three important Framers

George Washington, James Madison, and Benjamin Franklin were three important delegates to the convention.

Can you write a slogan for Washington's and Madison's T-shirts?

George Washington came from Virginia. He was probably the most respected man in the country. As commander-in-chief of the American army during the Revolution, he was a great hero to most people. Now he had retired to his plantation and would have liked to remain there. However, his friends told him he should attend the convention. They said his support was necessary to get a new constitution accepted by the people. Since Washington thought a stronger national government was necessary, he came to Philadelphia.

James Madison is often called the "Father of the Constitution." His ideas about government greatly influenced the other delegates. He had already developed a written plan for the new government which he brought to Philadelphia. It was known as the Virginia Plan and it called for a strong national government. Madison took notes during the meetings. Much of what we know about the Philadelphia Convention is based on his notes.

Benjamin Franklin attended the convention as a delegate from Pennsylvania. He was 81 years old and in poor health. Like Washington, he was highly respected by Americans. He had been a printer, inventor, and writer. He had also helped our country develop good relations with other nations. At the convention, he encouraged the delegates to cooperate with each other and work hard to settle their differences. His support of the Constitution was important to the other delegates.

Important Founders who were not at the convention

Some well-known Founders were not at the convention. Thomas Jefferson and Thomas Paine were in France. Jefferson had written the Declaration of Independence. Paine had written *Common Sense,* an important book that helped get support for the Revolution. John Adams was in Great Britain. He also had been a leader during the Revolution.

Some well-known Americans refused to go to the convention. Patrick Henry of Virginia was one of them. He said he "smelled a rat." He meant that he suspected the delegates would try to create a strong national government. Henry feared a strong national government. After the convention, Henry worked against **ratification** of the Constitution.

What was Patrick Henry afraid of?

ratification
approval

The convention begins

By May 25, 1787, delegates from over half of the states had arrived in Philadelphia. From the start, the Framers agreed on four things.

1. George Washington would serve as president of the convention.

2. Each state, large or small, would have one vote at the convention.

3. They would not follow the instructions Congress had given them. They would not even try to improve the Articles of Confederation. They thought the Articles had too many weaknesses. Instead, they decided to write an entirely new constitution.

Do you agree with the Framers' decision to keep their discussions private?

4. They would keep their discussions private. They also decided that what they said at the convention would remain a secret for 30 years. There were two reasons for this.

- They believed they needed to speak freely to create the best possible constitution. If people could listen to them and tell others what they said, they would not feel as free to discuss their ideas.

- They wanted the new constitution to be accepted by the people. They were afraid that the people might not accept it if they knew all the disagreements the Framers had.

Once the Framers reached these agreements, it was time to get down to work and create a constitution. In the next lessons you will learn about some of the disagreements the Framers had and how they solved them.

Reviewing and using the lesson

1. Why did Congress call for the Philadelphia Convention? Why was the purpose of the meeting changed?

2. In what ways were the delegates representative of the American people? In what ways were they not?

3. Why did the Framers decide to keep the convention debates a secret for so long? Pretend you are a newspaper editor in Philadelphia in 1787. Write an article in which you support or oppose keeping the debates secret.

4. Explain these terms: Philadelphia Convention, delegates, ratification.

LESSON 8

How many representatives should each state have in Congress?

Purpose of Lesson

The delegates to the Philadelphia Convention agreed that the Articles of Confederation needed to be replaced by a new constitution. They also agreed that the new constitution needed to provide for a stronger national government.

The Framers did not agree on everything. In this lesson and in the following lesson, you will learn about some differences among the delegates. This lesson describes the disagreement over how many representatives each state should be able to send to the new Congress.

population
the number of people living in an area

Problem solving

How many representatives should your state have?

Your class should act as delegates to the Philadelphia Convention. The class should be divided into committees of equal numbers—about six students each. Half of each committee should act as delegates from states with small **populations**. The other half should act as delegates from states with large populations. The task of each committee is to answer the following two questions:

1. How many representatives should each state be allowed to send to Congress?

2. How many votes should each state have in Congress?

After answering these questions, take the following steps:

- Each committee should write its answers on the chalkboard or chart paper so the rest of the class can read them.

- Each committee should explain the reasoning behind its answers.

- The class should discuss the answers and try to reach an agreement on the best answers to the questions.

- The class should then compare its answers with those of the Framers.

The conflict between the large and small states

How many representatives should each state be able to send to Congress? This was one of the most difficult questions the Framers had to answer.

Delegates from states with small populations were afraid. They did not want the larger states to have more votes in Congress than they had. If that happened, they were afraid the large states would control the new national government. Delegates from small states argued that each state should have the same number of representatives in Congress.

Delegates from states with large populations thought that was not fair. They believed that a state with more people should have more votes in Congress.

During the long debates, the Framers could not reach a decision on this issue. Neither side was willing to give in. The delegates were almost ready to quit and go home. A special committee of one delegate from each state was formed to try and find a solution.

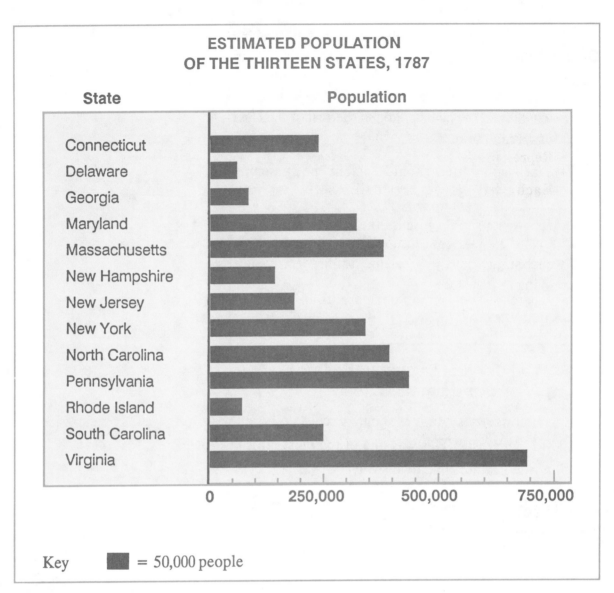

ESTIMATED POPULATION
OF THE THIRTEEN STATES, 1787

State — **Population**

Connecticut
Delaware
Georgia
Maryland
Massachusetts
New Hampshire
New Jersey
New York
North Carolina
Pennsylvania
Rhode Island
South Carolina
Virginia

0   250,000   500,000   750,000

Key ■ = 50,000 people

How could you organize Congress so each state would be represented fairly?

majority
more than half

The Great Compromise

Compromise is a way of dealing with a problem. Each side gives up something in order to reach a solution which is acceptable to both sides. The delegates knew they had to solve the problem of representation. The members of the committee worked hard to find a compromise a **majority** of the delegates would accept.

The result of the committee's work is known as the **Great Compromise**. The main parts of this compromise were:

- Congress would have two parts, or houses. These houses would be the **Senate** and the **House of Representatives**.

- Each state, large or small, would have two representatives in the Senate.

- In the House, the number of representatives of each state would be based on the number of people living in that state.

Virginia

New Jersey

Why do you think both the large and small states could agree on the Great Compromise?

THE SENATE

Virginia   Rhode Island

How are the interests of states with small populations protected?

HOUSE OF REPRESENTATIVES

Rhode Island

Virginia

How are the interests of states with large populations protected?

This agreement meant that each state would have equal power in the Senate. The states with more people would have more power in the House of Representatives. However, no law could be passed unless a majority of both the Senate and the House of Representatives voted for it. Because of this compromise, large and small states could check each other's power and protect their own interests.

There were many delegates who did not like the Great Compromise. It was hard for them to give up what they wanted. The Great Compromise passed by only one vote.

Reviewing and using the lesson

1. If the disagreement about representatives arose today, would you support the large states or the small states? Explain your answer.

2. How many representatives does your state have in the Senate? Who are they?

3. How many representatives does your state send to the House of Representatives? Who is your congressional representative?

4. Explain these terms: population, compromise, majority, Great Compromise, House of Representatives, Senate.

How should the problem of slavery be handled?

Purpose of Lesson

As you learned in the last lesson, the Framers had to compromise to solve their disagreements. The Great Compromise solved some of these differences. There were also disagreements between the Northern and Southern states about slavery. In this lesson you will learn how the Framers compromised to solve this disagreement.

What do you think the Framers believed about slavery?

Slavery in America

When our nation was founded, **slavery** had been practiced in many parts of the world for thousands of years. People in America had owned slaves from the time of the first British colonies. Black people were captured in Africa and sold to the colonists. Some Native Americans were also sold as slaves.

slavery
ownership of human beings as property

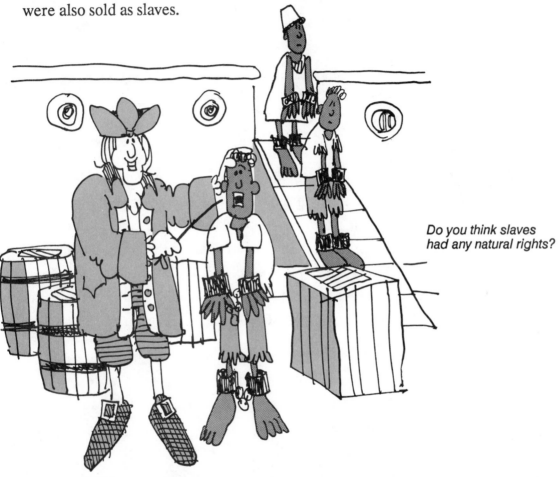

Do you think slaves had any natural rights?

Slaves were considered personal property that could be bought and sold. Slave families were often broken up, and children were sold separately from their parents. Slaves were not citizens and did not have any rights of citizens.

When the Declaration of Independence was written, there were about 500,000 slaves in the United States. There were slaves in almost every state, both North and South.

How did people in the North make their living?

People living in the Northern states made their living in a number of different ways. They worked as farmers, fishermen, merchants, and bankers. Others owned shops or worked in them. Most people in the North did not own slaves. They paid people to work for them. However, many Northerners made their living in the slave trade. They brought slaves from Africa and sold them to Southerners.

Most people in the Southern states were farmers. There were more slaves in the South because many farmers used slaves to work their lands.

What did the Framers think about slavery?

The Framers came to Philadelphia with different ideas about slavery. Many of the delegates, including some delegates from the South, believed slavery was wrong.

However, some Southern delegates wanted to protect the way many people in their states made their living. These delegates said they would not support the Constitution if it abolished slavery. They said their states would refuse to be part of the new national government. They wanted their citizens to have the right to own slaves and to bring in more slaves from other countries.

There were three main disagreements about slavery that had to be solved at the convention:

- Should the slave trade, which brought slaves from Africa to America, be allowed to continue?

- Should slaves be counted as part of a state's population? If this happened, it would allow the slave states to have more representatives in Congress. More representatives would give the Southern states more power.

- What should happen to slaves who ran away from their masters?

Let's look at how the Framers dealt with these disagreements.

What compromises did the Framers make?

After long arguments, the Framers agreed on several compromises about slavery. They were accepted by both the Northern and Southern states. The main purpose of these compromises was to get the Southern states to agree to be part of the new government. As with all compromises, neither side got everything it wanted.

- The Constitution allowed slavery to continue. Slaves who escaped to other states had to be returned to their owners. The national government was not allowed to stop people from importing slaves until 1808.

- In return, the Southern states agreed to something the Northern states wanted. Congress would have the power to control trade between the states which would help Northern businesses.

● Finally, Northern and Southern delegates agreed upon another compromise. It was called the **three-fifths clause**. It gave Southern states the right to count each slave as three-fifths of a person. This way the Southern states could send more representatives to Congress than if they were not allowed to count their slaves at all. However, it gave them fewer representatives than if they had been allowed to count each slave as one person.

What did the three-fifths clause do?

As a result of these compromises, the Southern delegates agreed to support the Constitution and to remain a part of the new nation.

The end of slavery

Neither side in the argument about slavery in Philadelphia represented the slaves themselves. Slavery continued in the United States for almost eighty years after the Constitution was written. It ended only as a result of the Civil War—the war between the Northern and Southern states.

Soon after the Civil War, the Constitution was changed to give the former slaves the rights of citizens. However, these changes in the Constitution did not end the problem of unfair treatment of the former slaves. You will learn more about this problem in Unit Four.

Why do you think a war was fought over slavery?

Reviewing and using the lesson

1. Why did the Northern and Southern delegates have different ideas about slavery?

2. How is the three-fifths clause an example of a compromise?

3. Pretend you are a delegate to the Philadelphia Convention. Write a letter home to your family in which you explain your position on the slavery question.

4. Explain these terms: slavery, three-fifths clause.

LESSON 10

What basic ideas are in the Preamble to the Constitution?

Purpose of Lesson

The Framers wrote an introduction, or preamble to the Constitution. The Preamble gives the purposes of our Constitution. It includes some of the basic ideas about government that you have studied earlier in this book. When you finish this lesson, you should be able to tell what these ideas mean.

What does the Preamble say?

The **Preamble** to the Constitution explains who created the Constitution and the basic purposes of our government.

"We the People..." are the first words in the Preamble. These words are very important. They show that the power to govern belongs to the people. The people established the Constitution. They used it to create a government to protect their rights and their welfare.

The Preamble's ideas

The ideas in the Preamble are so important that you should study them carefully. To do this, first read the entire Preamble.

Preamble to the Constitution
of the United States

We the People of the United States, in order to form a more perfect union, **establish justice, insure domestic tranquility, provide for the common defense, promote the general welfare, and secure the blessings of liberty** *to ourselves and our posterity, do ordain and establish this Constitution for the United States of America.*

You can see the Preamble contains a lot of words that are not easy to understand when you first read them. But, if you study them, you will find they are not that difficult.

What did the Framers mean when they wrote "insure domestic tranquility"?

71

What do these pictures tell you about the purpose of our Constitution?

Let's examine the basic ideas in the Preamble to see how important they are to all of us. To do this, your class should be divided into six groups. Each group should study one of the important parts of the Preamble listed below.

Important parts of the Preamble

Group 1. We the People...do ordain and establish this Constitution for the United States of America.

Group 2. establish justice...

Group 3. insure domestic tranquility...

Group 4. provide for the common defense...

Group 5. promote the general welfare...

Group 6. secure the blessings of liberty...

Each group should answer the following questions about the part it is studying. Be prepared to explain your group's answers to the rest of the class.

1. What does the part mean? Give an example.

2. Why is it important?

3. What does it have to do with protecting your rights and welfare?

Reviewing and using the lesson

1. What basic ideas about the purposes of our government are included in the Preamble?

2. Some people have said the most important words in our Constitution are the first three words of the Preamble. These are the words, *"We the People..."* Explain why you agree or disagree with this opinion.

3. Explain these terms: Preamble, justice, domestic tranquility, common defense, general welfare.

Unit Three

How did the Framers organize our government?

How does the Constitution make sure our government serves the people?

When the Framers wrote our Constitution they used a very important idea: **Government is the servant of the people. It is not the master of the people.**

We the people create our government. We give it the power to govern the nation for us.

However, we keep the right to control our government. We can control our government by voting and other ways that are protected by the Constitution. The people we choose to work for us in our government are our servants, not our masters.

In most other nations in 1787, the government was the master of the people. The government held all the power. Even today, many governments are still the masters of their people. People living under these governments have very few of the rights we have.

The Framers knew when they created our government that they faced a difficult problem. They wanted to create a stronger national government. But they also worried about creating a government with too much power. A government with too much power might become our master instead of our servant.

Try to imagine how you would solve this problem if you were one of the Framers. Suppose you were creating a new government for our country. You know you have to give the government power over your life, liberty, and property. You are afraid of giving the government so much power.

How can you plan your government so it will remain the servant of the people? How can you organize it so its powers will be limited and it will not become your master? In this unit, you will learn how the Framers solved this problem.

How did the Framers limit the powers of our government?

Purpose of Lesson

In this lesson you will learn some new ideas the Framers used to limit the powers of the national government. The Framers wanted to be sure that no one group of people would have too much power. So they divided the powers of the government. This lesson will help you understand the ideas of separation of powers and checks and balances.

Problem solving

How would you organize your government?

Suppose you were going to create a government for your class. Think how you would organize that government. It would need to have the following powers:

1. **Power to make rules.** This power is called **legislative** power.

2. **Power to carry out the rules.** This power is called **executive** power.

3. **Power to settle disagreements over the rules.** This power is called **judicial** power. Judicial power includes the power to say what the rules mean.

Now think about how you would distribute these powers. Work in groups of three to five students to answer the following questions. Be prepared to share your answers with the class.

SEPARATION OF POWERS

Judicial

Legislative

Executive

1. Suppose you gave all the above powers to one group of students. What would be the advantages and disadvantages of doing this?

2. Suppose you had three groups of students and divided the powers of your government among them. What would be the advantages and disadvantages of separating power this way?

What ideas did the Framers use?

When you answered these questions, you may have used some of the same ideas the Framers used. When they organized our government, they knew they needed to limit its powers. To understand how they did this, you will need to learn some new ideas. These are the ideas of **separation of powers** and **checks and balances**.

separation of powers
division of powers among the different branches of government

checks and balances
sharing and balancing of power among the different branches of government

Separation of powers

The Framers knew that constitutional governments are often divided into different parts or **branches**. Each branch is given certain powers. The Framers **separated the powers** of our government among three branches.

- **Legislative branch**. The Framers gave this branch the power to make laws. Our national legislature is called **Congress**. Congress has two parts or houses. They are the **Senate** and the **House of Representatives**.

- **Executive branch**. The Framers gave this branch the power to **enforce**, or carry out, the laws made by Congress. The **President** is the head of this branch.

- **Judicial branch**. The Framers gave this branch the power to settle disagreements about what our laws mean. The **Supreme Court** is the highest court in this branch.

The Framers knew that separation of powers among the different branches is one way to limit the powers of a government.

Balancing powers

The Framers also knew that it was not enough just to separate the powers of government. If you gave too much power to one branch of government, it might control the others. The Framers believed that the powers of government needed to be balanced among the different branches. **Balancing the powers** of government means that no one branch is given so much power it can completely control the other branches.

Legislative

Judicial

Executive

How does our Constitution separate and balance the powers of the government?

Checking powers

Once powers are separated and balanced, there is still another way to limit power. Each branch of government can be given checks on the other branches. For example, under the Constitution, the President can **check** the power of Congress by refusing to approve a bill it has passed. Such a bill will not become a law unless two-thirds of the members of Congress vote to make it a law. In the following lessons, you will learn about other checks and balances the Framers placed in the Constitution.

Why did the Framers organize our government this way?

The Framers knew that governments often gain too much power. When they do, they usually violate the rights of the people. They work for the selfish interests of a few people instead of for the common welfare.

The Framers wanted to make sure this could not happen. They separated the powers among the different branches. They balanced the powers among these branches. They gave each branch a way to check the use of power by the other branches.

The Framers believed the way they organized our government was the best way to protect our rights and our welfare.

Reviewing and using the lesson

1. What branches does our government have? What powers are given to each branch?

2. Why did the Framers separate the powers of our government? How are they separated?

3. Why did the Framers balance the powers of our government?

4. Why did the Framers provide ways each branch of our government can check the powers of the other branches? Give an example of how this is done.

5. How are powers separated in your school?

6. Explain these terms: separation of powers, checks and balances, legislative branch, executive branch, enforce, judicial branch.

What is the legislative branch?

What is Congress?

Congress makes our nation's laws. As you have learned, the Framers created two houses of Congress, the Senate and the House of Representatives.

You may remember that the Framers disagreed over how many representatives each state could send to Congress. They solved this disagreement by the Great Compromise. The compromise was as follows:

- **Senate.** Each state can send two representatives to the Senate. Our Senate now has 100 members.

- **House of Representatives.** The number of representatives each state can send to the House of Representatives is based upon its population. For example, in 1988, California, which has the largest population, had 45 representatives. Wyoming, Delaware, North Dakota and South Dakota, with the smallest population, had one representative each. Our House of Representatives now has 435 members.

What are the powers of Congress?

Article I of the Constitution contains a long list of the powers of Congress. Some of these powers are very specific. For example, Congress has the power to tax the people, to create a court system, and to declare war.

Other powers of Congress are very general. For example, the Constitution also gives Congress the power to pass all laws that are necessary to carry out its responsibilities. Congress is responsible for providing for the general welfare of the United States. What do you think this means? How does Congress provide for the welfare of our country?

What does the legislative branch do?

How does Congress make a law?

Congress provides for the common welfare by passing laws that it thinks will help people. Suppose your member of the House of Representatives has an idea for a new law. How does the member get his or her idea made into a law?

The following is a simplified version of some basic steps your representative must follow to create a law.

1. **Write a bill.** The member must write the idea down. This written idea is called a **bill.**

2. **Get a majority vote of Congress.** The member must get a majority of members of the House of Representatives to vote for the bill. Then, a majority of members of the Senate must also vote for the bill.

3. **Get the President to approve the bill.** Finally, the bill must be sent to the President. If the President approves the bill and signs it, it becomes a **law.** If the President **vetoes** the bill, then it can only become a law if two-thirds of the members of Congress vote for it.

bill
a proposed law sent to the legislature for approval

law
a bill that has been passed by both houses of Congress and signed by the President

veto
power of the President to refuse to approve a bill passed by Congress

What are the responsibilities of your members of Congress?

The main job of your members of Congress is to help make our nation's laws. Members of Congress are responsible for making laws that protect our rights and promote our welfare.

To make laws, members of Congress must learn about the problems of the country and find ways to solve them. Members of Congress study our nation's problems. They talk to many people. They read letters written by the people they represent. They listen to debates and attend committee meetings.

83

Making good laws is not easy. Members of Congress have to decide whether or not to support each bill. Some bills might help some people, but hurt others. The following activity will help you see how difficult it can be to decide whether to support a bill.

Problem solving

How should Senator Smith vote?

Pretend Senator Smith is going to visit your community to ask your advice on the problem described below. Your class should be divided into groups of three to five students. One group should take the role of Senator Smith and her staff members. The other groups should represent people in Senator Smith's state. Each group should read the story on the next page and answer the questions that follow it.

After all groups have finished their assignment, the class should hold a public hearing. Each of the groups should tell Senator Smith how it thinks she should vote. Then Senator Smith and her staff should discuss the problem, decide what to do, and explain their decision to the class.

Senator Smith has to decide

Smoking cigarettes is a national problem. Studies have shown that smoking is very dangerous to your health. Even breathing smoke from someone else's cigarette is dangerous. Each year thousands of Americans die from smoking cigarettes.

Senator Smith represents a state in which tobacco is a very important crop. Many people in her state are involved either in growing tobacco or making cigarettes. A bill is in Congress that would prohibit people from smoking in public places.

Senator Smith believes smoking is dangerous to people's health. She thinks it would be better if people are not allowed to smoke in public places. However, if she votes for the bill, the tobacco industry will be hurt. Many people in her state will lose their jobs.

Senator Smith has to decide how to vote on the bill. Should she vote against the bill to protect the jobs of the people in her state? Should she vote for the bill because she believes smoking is dangerous to people's health?

- Senator Smith is supposed to support laws that protect people's rights.

  - What rights are involved in this situation?
  - Which rights do you think are most important? Why?

- What is the common welfare in this situation? Explain your answer.

- How do you think Senator Smith should vote? Explain your position.

Whose interests should Senator Smith protect?

How are the powers of Congress limited?

The powers of Congress are limited. Congress cannot make any law it wishes and have the law enforced. For example, Congress cannot make a law that unfairly limits your basic rights.

Suppose Congress voted for a bill that said if you did not believe in a certain religion, you could not vote. If the President approved such a bill, it would become a law. How could this law be stopped to protect your rights?

The Supreme Court has the power to declare a law made by Congress **unconstitutional**. The Court may say that the Constitution does not give Congress the right to pass such a law. If the Supreme Court says this, the law may not be enforced.

unconstitutional
not allowed by the Constitution

Reviewing and using the lesson

1. What are the qualifications for members of the Senate and the House of Representatives?

   To answer this question, look at the copy of the Constitution in this text. Find Article I. Under Article I, find Section Two. Read the qualifications for members of the House of Representatives. To find the qualifications for Senators, read Article I, Section Three.

2. Find and explain one of the powers of Congress listed in the Constitution. To do this, look at Article I, Section Eight of the Constitution.

3. Who are the two senators from your state? Who represents you in the House of Representatives? If you don't know, where do you think you can find this information?

4. Find an article in the newspaper that explains something Congress is doing. Be prepared to explain the article to your class.

5. Explain these terms: bill, law, veto, unconstitutional.

LESSON 13

What is the executive branch?

Purpose of Lesson

The Framers created the executive branch to carry out the laws passed by Congress. The President is the head of the executive branch. In this lesson you will learn about the powers of the President. You will also read how these powers are checked and balanced by those of Congress.

Creating the executive branch

The Framers had many discussions about how much power to give the executive branch. They did not want to make it too weak or too strong. The Framers wanted to do two things.

1. They wanted to give the President enough power to carry out and enforce the laws made by Congress.

2. They did not want to give the President too much power. If they did, a President might be able to gain unlimited power and become a dictator.

What are the powers of the President?

The Framers gave the President many powers and responsibilities as head of our nation. The duties and powers of the President are listed in Article II of the Constitution. Some of these powers are:

- The President is the head of the executive branch.

- The President is commander-in-chief of the armed forces.
- The President is responsible for dealing with other countries.

The President is the single most powerful person in our government.

What are the responsibilities of the executive branch?

CONGRESS

How can Congress limit the
powers of the President?

How are the powers of the President limited by Congress?

The Framers were careful to limit the powers of the President. They did this by making the President share most powers with Congress. Here are some examples of how the powers of the President can be checked by Congress.

- **Appointments.** The President has the power to appoint people to important jobs in the executive and judicial branches. However, the Senate can limit or check this power by not approving the persons suggested by the President.

- **Treaties.** The President has the power to make a treaty with another nation. However, the treaty must be approved by the Senate.

- **War.** The President can **conduct** a war. However, only Congress can **declare** a war. Although the President commands the armed forces, Congress can check this power by controlling the money needed to conduct a war.

- **Veto.** By a two-thirds vote, Congress may approve a bill over the President's veto.

- **Impeachment.** The Constitution gives Congress the power to **impeach** the President. If found guilty, the President can be removed from office.

impeach
to charge with a crime

In the next lesson, you will learn how the Supreme Court can check the President's power.

What happens if the President vetoes a bill passed by Congress?

George Washington was our first President

In 1789 George Washington was elected to be our first President. It was hard for people to imagine what a president would be like. Americans had never had a president before. Even Congress did not know what they should call him. Some people thought the President should be called "Your Majesty." Congress disagreed. America was ruled by the people, not by a king. So Congress decided to call Washington simply "The President of the United States."

Read the following story and answer the questions that follow. The story shows how hard it was for many people to realize that the President's power comes from the people. Remember that in 1790 most people in the world were ruled by kings.

Peter and President Washington

Ever since coming to the United States from his home in Vienna, Peter had looked forward to this day. His father, the ambassador, had made a special appointment for him to meet George Washington, the President of the United States.

Peter and his father went into the President's office. Peter bowed and said, "Your Excellency."

The President smiled and shook his head. "Oh, no, Peter. You must not bow. And you do not need to call me 'Excellency.' Just call me 'Mr. President.'"

Peter was confused. He had learned to bow before the king as a sign of respect. Was not George Washington a king? Was president another word for king? He decided to ask another question.

"Mr. President," Peter began again, "when I met the King of Prussia, he said that he learned to be a king from his father. His father had been king before him. Did you learn to be president from your father? Will your son also be president after you?"

"I am not a king," said President Washington. "I do not have a son. But if I did, he could only be president if he were elected by the people. Presidents of the United States do not get their powers from their fathers or mothers as kings and queens do. My powers come from an important document called the Constitution."

The President pulled a book from the shelf and handed it to Peter. "Read this," he said. "The first three words of the Preamble tell you where the Constitution gets its power."

Peter read aloud, "We the People of the United States ...."

"You see, Peter," said the President, "the Constitution's power, my power, and all the powers of our government come from an agreement of the people. This is the basis for our government."

1. Where did President Washington say the powers of our Constitution come from?

2. Where did President Washington say his powers came from?

3. What basic ideas that you have studied are included in this story?

How is the executive branch organized?

The Framers knew the President would need help in running the executive branch. However, they did not plan how to organize the executive branch. The Framers left it up to Congress and President Washington to organize the first executive branch.

The first Congress created a number of departments to help the President. The people in charge of these departments were called **secretaries**. They acted as advisers to the President and became known as his **cabinet**.

The first cabinet had four members. Today the cabinet has thirteen members. In fact, the entire executive branch has grown far beyond anything the Framers could have imagined. More people now work for the executive branch than lived in all the colonies at the time of the Revolution!

secretaries
heads of the departments of the executive branch

cabinet
a group made up of the secretaries of government departments who act as advisers to the President

Reviewing and using the lesson

1. What qualifications must a person meet to be President? To answer this question, see the Constitution, Article II, Section One, part 5.

2. Explain one of the powers of the President. To do this, see Article II, Section Two.

3. What is the President's cabinet?

4. Explain two ways the President's powers can be limited.

5. Who is the President today?

6. Find an article in the newspaper that explains something the President is doing. Be prepared to explain the article to your class.

7. Explain these terms: impeach, secretaries, cabinet.

What is the judicial branch?

Purpose of Lesson

The Framers created the judicial branch to handle disagreements over the law. Article III of our Constitution describes the responsibilities and powers of this branch. In this lesson, you will learn how the judicial branch works.

What does the judicial branch do?

Suppose you thought the government had taken away one of your rights guaranteed by the Constitution. What could you do? You could ask the judicial branch to protect your rights. You could ask a court to listen to your case. If the court agreed with you, it would order the government to stop what it was doing and protect your rights.

What does the judicial branch do?

95

interpret
explain the meaning of the law

The courts **interpret** the law. They also settle disagreements between individuals and the government. Different levels of courts handle different kinds of cases. Federal courts handle cases about the Constitution and the laws made by Congress. They also deal with problems between one or more states.

How is the judicial branch organized?

The **Supreme Court** is the highest court in the judicial branch. The judicial branch also includes lower courts. The judges on the Supreme Court are called **justices**. The head of the Supreme Court is the **Chief Justice**.

The Framers believed that if judges were elected by the people, they might favor some people over others. For this reason, judges are not elected. They are appointed to office. Judges on all federal courts are appointed by the President. However, the Senate must approve all the President's appointments. Judges serve in the judicial branch until they retire or die. They can also be impeached, tried, and removed from their positions, just like the President.

How many justices are on the U.S. Supreme Court? Can you name any of them?

What is judicial review?

Judicial review is one of the most important powers of the judicial branch. Judicial review is the power of the courts to say that the Constitution does not allow the government to do something. For example, the Supreme Court can say that a law passed by Congress is not constitutional. The Supreme Court can also say that the President is not allowed to do certain things.

Suppose Congress passed a law that said you must belong to a certain religion. The Constitution says Congress cannot do this. You can go to court and say that Congress has no right to tell you to belong to a certain religion. The court will review your case. The court has the power to say that the law made by Congress is unconstitutional. If the court does this, the law cannot be enforced.

When you read the following story, you will see how the Supreme Court used its power of judicial review. In this case, the Court decided a state law was unconstitutional.

Torcaso v. Watkins (1961)

The State of Maryland had a law saying that everyone who wanted a job in the state government had to swear that he or she believed in God. A man named Torcaso applied for a job as a government official. He was denied the job because he would not say that he believed in God.

Mr. Torcaso said that the Maryland law was unconstitutional because it limited his freedom of religion. He said that freedom of religion meant the freedom to believe in God or not to believe in God, as a person wishes.

The Supreme Court agreed with Mr. Torcaso. The Court said the Maryland law was unconstitutional and could not be enforced. The Court ruled that people cannot be required to say that they believe in God or do not believe in God.

The Supreme Court was using its power of judicial review over the action of a state government.

Why is judicial review important?

Reviewing and using the lesson

1. What court is the highest court in the judicial branch?

2. Why are Supreme Court justices appointed and not elected? Do you agree with this system? Why or why not?

3. Do you think the Supreme Court should have the power to declare a law made by majority vote in Congress to be unconstitutional? Why or why not?

4. Find an article in the newspaper that explains something the Supreme Court is doing. Be prepared to explain the article to your class.

5. Explain these terms: interpret, Supreme Court, justices, Chief Justice, judicial review.

What is a federal government?

Purpose of Lesson

When they wrote the Constitution, the Framers created a new kind of government. It is called a federal system. When you finish this lesson, you should be able to explain what a federal system is. You should know some of its strengths and weaknesses. Finally, you should be able to explain why you think the Framers created this type of government.

Problem solving

What is a federal system?

When the Framers wrote our Constitution, they created a **federal system** of government. In a federal system, the people do not give all the power to the national government. Instead, they give some powers to their national government and some powers to their state and city governments. Finally, the people keep some powers and rights for themselves.

The illustration on the next page shows how our federal system of government works. Look at the illustration and answer the questions below. Then share your answers with the rest of the class.

- Where does power come from in this system of government?

- To whom is power given?

- Why do you think the Framers chose this system of government?

What does this picture tell you about our federal system?

Where have the people placed the power?

The following are examples of how we, the people, give power to different parts of our government.

- **Powers to the national (federal) government.** We give some powers to our national government. Examples are the power to:
  - tax the people to support the national government
  - create post offices
  - control trade between states and trade with other nations
  - declare and conduct war
  - create money
- **Powers to the state governments.** We give some powers to our state governments. Examples are the power to:
  - tax the people to support the state government
  - create public schools
  - make motor vehicle laws

- make laws regulating marriage and divorce
- control trade within our state
- **Powers kept by the people.** We keep certain powers and rights for ourselves. These include rights such as:
  - believing what we wish
  - selecting our careers
  - choosing our friends
  - traveling where we wish to go

In our federal system, the national and state governments **share** certain powers. For example, both governments have the power to tax the people. Both governments have the power to provide for the health and welfare of the people.

The powers of the federal government are greater than those of the state

The Framers wrote, "This Constitution, and the laws of the United States ... shall be the **supreme law of the land....**" This statement means that the states cannot make laws that conflict with the Constitution. States also cannot make laws that conflict with laws made by Congress.

Why do you think the Framers gave the federal government greater powers than they gave the states?

Limiting government to protect our rights

You now understand more about how the Framers organized our government. We have a national government. We have state governments. We also have local governments of our towns and cities.

101

Many Framers believed that this way of organizing our government was enough to protect our rights. However, some Americans were still worried. They thought the new Constitution gave too much power to the national government. They refused to accept the Constitution unless a bill of rights was added to it.

Bill of Rights
the first ten amendments to the Constitution

The **Bill of Rights** was another way to limit the powers of the national government. It was another way to protect our rights. You will learn about the Bill of Rights in the next unit.

Reviewing and using the lesson

1. Explain what a federal system is. Draw a cartoon or chart that shows how the federal system works in the United States.

2. Suppose you, like the Framers, were organizing a government.

   - Explain what you think might be some of the advantages and disadvantages of a federal system of government.

   - Which powers would you give to the federal government? Why?

   - Which powers would you give to the state governments? Why?

   - Which powers would you keep for yourselves? Why?

3. Look in a newspaper and find examples of the use of power by federal, state, and local governments. Be prepared to explain the examples to your class.

4. Explain these terms: federal system, supreme law of the land, Bill of Rights.

Unit Four

How does the Constitution protect your basic rights?

What are some of our basic rights protected by the Constitution?

When the Constitution was written, many Founders were worried that the rights of the people were not protected enough. They said they would only help to get the Constitution ratified if a bill of rights was added when the first Congress met. The other Founders agreed, and that is exactly what happened.

The **Bill of Rights** is the name for the first ten **amendments** added to the Constitution. It is a part of the Constitution. The Bill of Rights was adopted in 1791, four years after the original Constitution was adopted. Since that time, other amendments have been added. Most have given rights to people who were not given these rights in the original Constitution. For example, the 19th Amendment, added in 1920, gave women the right to vote.

amendments
changes and additions

The Bill of Rights protected people's rights from interference by the **national** government. The Bill of Rights did not apply to the **state** governments. After the Civil War, this situation changed. Amendments were added to the Constitution to protect people's rights from unfair actions by state governments. Today, all the important rights of the Bill of Rights are protected from unfair actions by either the national or the state governments.

In this unit you will learn how your basic rights are protected under the Constitution, the Bill of Rights, and later amendments. You will also learn how the Constitution now protects the rights of people who were denied them in the past.

We will not study all the amendments and parts of the Constitution that protect your rights. Instead, we will study five basic rights protected by the Constitution. These are:

1. **The right to freedom of expression.** The Constitution protects your right to express your ideas. It also protects your right to learn about the ideas of other people.

2. **The right to freedom of religion.** The Constitution protects your right to believe in any or no religion. It also protects your right to practice your religious beliefs.

3. **The right to be treated equally.** The Constitution does not allow the government to favor some groups of people over others.

4. **The right to be treated fairly.** The Constitution does not allow the government to make unfair and unreasonable laws. The government also cannot be unfair to you in the ways it carries out and enforces the law.

5. **The right to vote.** The Constitution says everyone eighteen years old or older has the right to vote.

These rights are important to you and to all of us living in the United States. You will learn more about these rights and their importance in this unit.

How does the Constitution protect your freedom of expression?

Purpose of Lesson

In this lesson, you will learn why freedom of expression was important to the Founders. You also will learn why it is so important today, both to you and to our nation. When you have completed this lesson, you should be able to explain the benefits of freedom of expression. You should also be able to explain when it might be reasonable to limit this freedom.

What is freedom of expression?

Suppose someone asked you to make a list of some of the freedoms you think are very important. Most Americans would say they think it is important to have freedom of:

- **speech** - the right to say whatever they wish to say

- **press** - the right to read and write whatever they wish

- **assembly** - the right to meet with others to talk about whatever they wish

- **petition** - the right to ask the government to correct things that they think are wrong

These rights—freedom of **speech, press, assembly,** and **petition**—are part of the right to **freedom of expression.** Our right to freedom of expression is protected by the First Amendment of the Bill of Rights.

How does the Bill of Rights protect freedom of speech?

Our Constitution limits the powers of our government in order to protect these freedoms. Under our Constitution, the government cannot interfere with these rights except under very special circumstances.

What are the benefits of freedom of expression?

Freedom of expression is important to us as individuals and as citizens. The following are some of the reasons it is so important.

- **Freedom of expression supports our democracy.** Our democratic system of government depends on the people's ability to make good decisions. To make good decisions, you need to be able to get enough information to make up your mind. You need to hear and discuss different ideas and opinions. When you are able to vote, discussing different points of view will help you decide which are the best people or laws to vote for.

Why is it important to be able to exchange ideas freely?

- **Freedom of expression helps us grow as individuals.** When you express your thoughts and listen to the ideas of others, you learn and become more mature. Hearing and discussing different points of view helps you make thoughtful choices about what you think is right. You mature as a person when you make choices for yourself rather than just accepting what others tell you.

- **Freedom of expression advances knowledge.** It is easier for you to make new discoveries and gain new knowledge when you can suggest ideas and exchange information freely. Even if some ideas do not work, they provide a way of testing the truth of other ideas.

- **Freedom of expression makes peaceful change in society possible.** If you are free to try to persuade others to change things, you are less likely to use violence. We have improved many things in our country by using our right to freedom of expression. And, if we can criticize things we can't change, we may be willing to accept them until we can get them changed.

Why is it necessary to protect freedom of expression?

The Founders of our nation knew it was necessary to protect freedom of expression. Throughout history governments had often tried to stop people from spreading new ideas or criticizing government actions.

For example, the Founders knew that in the American colonies, people had suffered—and sometimes died—for saying what they thought. In the Massachusetts Colony in 1660, a woman named Mary Dyer had been hanged by the Puritans for teaching that slavery, war, and **capital punishment** were evil.

capital punishment
*death as a legal
punishment for a crime*

107

What do you think the Founders learned from the experiences of people like Mary Dyer?

That is why the Founders insisted that freedom of expression be protected in the Constitution.

Should freedom of expression ever be limited?

As you have learned, our democracy depends on freedom of expression. However, sometimes it is fair to limit freedom of expression to protect other rights. For example, you may not cry "Fire!" in a crowded theater when there is no fire, just to frighten people. Someone might be hurt rushing to get out.

You are also not allowed to tell military secrets to foreign countries. This could be dangerous for the entire nation.

Can you think of any other situations in which it might be fair to limit freedom of expression?

When do you think the government should have the right to limit your freedom of expression?

Problem solving

When should freedom of expression be limited?

Read the situation below. Then, in small groups, discuss answers to the questions that follow it. Be prepared to present your answers to the class.

One morning in 1961 about 200 black high school and college students met in front of a church in Columbia, South Carolina. They planned to walk to the State House and march around it carrying signs protesting unfair treatment. Some of the signs said, "Down with **segregation!**"

segregation
separation of people in public places because of their race

When the group reached the State House they walked back and forth carrying their signs. They did not stop traffic or block the sidewalks. After a few hours, about 200 to 300 people gathered to watch the students. Some were unfriendly to the students. The police, fearing trouble, told the students they would be arrested if they did not leave within fifteen minutes. The students did not leave. They listened to a speech by one of their leaders. Then they sang the "Star Spangled Banner" and other patriotic songs.

The police arrested 187 of the students and took them to jail. The students were tried and convicted of disturbing the peace. They were fined and given sentences of 5 to 30 days in jail.

The students said that their rights to freedom of speech and assembly had been taken unfairly from them. They appealed their convictions to the Supreme Court.

1. Should groups of people be allowed to do what these students did? Why or why not?

2. How are speaking and carrying signs the same?

3. Should the police be allowed to stop people from speaking or carrying signs if the people watching them become angry? Why or why not?

4. Suppose a small group of people in an audience get angry at a speaker and try to stop the person from speaking. Whose rights should the police protect? Give the reasons for your answer.

Reviewing and using the lesson

1. What types of expression are protected by the First Amendment? Give examples of each type you mention.

2. Which of the four benefits of free expression described in this lesson do you think is most important? Why? Give an example.

3. In what kinds of situations do you think it is fair and reasonable to limit freedom of expression? Give examples.

4. What advantages are there to letting everyone speak or write his or her ideas? What disadvantages?

5. Explain these terms: freedom of expression, capital punishment, segregation.

How does the Constitution protect your freedom of religion?

Purpose of Lesson

The Founders thought your right to freedom of religion was so important they placed it at the beginning of the Bill of Rights. In this lesson, you will learn why the Founders thought this freedom was so important. You will learn how the Constitution protects religious freedom. You will also study about situations in which religious freedom may be limited when it conflicts with other important rights and interests.

When you have finished this lesson, you should be able to explain the importance of freedom of religion. You should also be able to explain when it might be reasonable to limit this freedom.

The First Amendment protects freedom of religion

The very first words of the Bill of Rights protect your right to freedom of religion. They say, "Congress shall make no law respecting an establishment of religion, or prohibiting the free exercise thereof." These words show how important freedom of religion was to the Founders.

The words mean that Congress may not **establish** or set up any religion as the country's official religion. They also mean that Congress cannot prevent you from holding any religious beliefs you choose or from having no religious beliefs at all. Within reasonable limitations, you may **freely exercise** or practice any religious beliefs you wish.

Why was freedom of religion so important to the Founders?

Most of the early American colonists were Protestants. Few of the colonies allowed religious freedom. In several colonies, one Protestant religious group controlled the colony and made everyone go along with its ideas. People who disagreed were often **persecuted**. Some were even executed for their beliefs. Others were forced to leave the colony.

For example, Roger and Mary Williams and some of their followers were driven out of the Massachusetts Bay Colony. They founded the colony of Rhode Island where they could be free to practice their religion.

persecute
to cause suffering to a person or group because of their beliefs

By the end of the American Revolution, however, there were many more people who had different religious beliefs. Quakers, Catholics, Baptists, Jews, and members of many other religious groups lived in the new states. They believed they should have just as much right to practice their religious beliefs as anyone else.

Why did the Framers think it was necessary to protect religious freedom?

As a result, Americans got used to living with people of different religious beliefs. People began to believe that others should have the same rights they wanted for themselves.

Important leaders such as Thomas Jefferson and James Madison thought it was unfair to discriminate against people because of their religious beliefs. They thought such actions took away people's rights and were dangerous to the common welfare.

Most of the Founders were religious men and women. At the same time, they believed strongly that government should not interfere with people's right to practice different religions. George Washington, for example, believed that religion was necessary for the development of good character. However, he was against the use of tax money for the teaching of religion in public schools.

The Founders' strong belief in religious freedom led them to protect it first and foremost in the First Amendment.

Conflicts over the freedom-of-religion clauses

Your right to freedom of religion is protected by the Constitution. However, there have been disagreements over exactly what this freedom means. For example, the Constitution says that the government may not **establish** religion. Does this mean that public schools may not have prayers in the classroom? This question was raised in a case in 1962 that involved schools in a city in New York.

Problem solving

Prayer in the public schools

Read about the following situation. Then, in small groups of three to five students, answer the questions that follow it. Be prepared to share your answers with the class.

In 1958, the Board of Education in New Hyde Park, New York, gave the school district's principals a prayer. Teachers were required to lead students in saying the prayer out loud every day. Students who did not want to say the prayer were allowed to sit quietly or leave the room.

The parents of ten students complained. They said the use of this prayer in public schools was against their religious beliefs. They said that prayer was something people should do at home and in the church. They also said that to have such prayers in school put pressure on students to say the prayer. Students who did not say the prayer might be criticized by the other students. The parents took the case to court.

1. Suppose your teacher began each day by leading the class in saying a prayer out loud. Would this violate your right to believe in any religion you wish or to believe in no religion at all? Why or why not?

2. Teachers in this school system were paid by tax money collected from the citizens of New York. Does this mean that the government was supporting religion? Why or why not?

3. Do you think it is all right for the government to support religion if it helps all religions equally? Why or why not?

4. Do you think the Board of Education violated the Constitution? Why or why not?

Should public schools be allowed to set aside time for prayer?

Can the government limit your right to believe as you wish?

The First Amendment says that Congress shall make no law "prohibiting the **free exercise**..." of religion. These words mean that the government cannot interfere with your right to believe as you wish. You may believe in any religion you wish, or in no religion at all. The government may not interfere with your beliefs. For example, the government may not force you to swear to a belief you do not hold. You may not be forced to say a prayer in school.

Can the government limit your right to practice your beliefs?

The First Amendment also protects your right to practice your beliefs. However, this right can be limited if your religious practices are considered harmful to public health or the common welfare.

For example, suppose you believe in a religion that is against vaccination. You still may be required to be vaccinated against certain diseases before being admitted to school. Vaccination is required to protect everyone.

Other religious practices also may be forbidden, such as handling rattlesnakes as part of a religious ceremony. Most people consider such limitations to be reasonable.

Not everyone agrees with all the limitations placed upon religious practices. You will often hear differences of opinion about this subject. In our country, people have the right to hold different opinions. They have the right to try to get laws changed to protect their particular religious practices. They also have the right to argue their positions in our courts.

Should the government be allowed to require that you be vaccinated before you go to school?

Does freedom of religion allow you to shout your views in the middle of the night?

Reviewing and using the lesson

1. Why did the Framers believe it was important to include the protection of religious freedom in the Constitution?

2. Explain what is meant by the First Amendment when it says: "Congress shall make no law respecting an establishment of religion, or prohibiting the free exercise thereof."

3. Suppose there is a religious group that believes in human sacrifice. Should that group be allowed to practice its beliefs? Why or why not?

4. Should a person who does not believe in God have the same right to work for the government as someone who does believe? Why or why not?

5. Suppose there is a religious group that believes in shouting their prayers in the street at night when people are sleeping. Should they be arrested for disturbing the peace? Why or why not?

6. Should your government use the taxes collected from citizens to help any religions? Why or why not?

7. Should the government allow public school buildings to be used for religious teaching after school? Why or why not?

8. Explain these terms: persecute, free exercise.

How does the Constitution protect your right to be treated equally by the government?

Purpose of Lesson

The Fourteenth Amendment is one of the most important parts of the Constitution. One part of the Fourteenth Amendment has been used to protect people from unequal treatment by our government. This part is the equal protection clause. In this lesson, you will learn how this clause has been used to prevent states from being unfair to citizens because of their race.

Problem solving

What is equal treatment?

In small groups of three to five students, discuss each of the imaginary situations described below. Decide in each situation whether you think the government was being unfair to someone. Be prepared to share your opinions with the class.

1. Your state has a law that says students of your race must go to different schools from those attended by students of another race.

2. Your town has a law that says your family cannot live in a certain section of town because of your religion.

3. Your state has a law that says you cannot marry someone of a different race.

4. Your city police department will not allow women on the police force.

5. A man and woman work for the state government at the same jobs. Yet the man is paid much more than the woman.

Do you think people should get equal pay for doing the same work?

discrimination
unfair treatment of people because of their race, religion, or sex

equal protection
treating all people equally under the law

The Fourteenth Amendment and equal protection

The Fourteenth Amendment was passed to stop state governments from unfairly **discriminating** against black Americans. It says, "No State shall . . . deny to any person . . . the **equal protection of the laws.**" This means that states must not treat people unequally unless there is a good and fair reason for doing so.

However, just passing the Fourteenth Amendment did not stop unfair treatment of black people. States still passed laws that unfairly discriminated against them. For example, some states had separate schools for black and white children. Blacks often were not allowed to sit next to whites on trains or buses or to use the same public parks or swimming pools.

Many people thought these laws were unfair. They said the states were violating the Fourteenth Amendment. In 1896 some people asked the Supreme Court to rule that these laws were unconstitutional. At that time, the Supreme Court refused to do so. The Court said it was not unfair for states to separate white and black people. States could require blacks and whites to be separated in public places if the public places for each group were equal.

How did separate drinking fountains deny blacks equal protection?

Over the years, Americans' ideas about fairness and equality began to change. In 1954, the Supreme Court changed its interpretation of the equal protection clause. The Court decided one of the most important cases in our country's history.

What is the importance of the case of *Brown v. Board of Education*?

Linda Brown was seven years old. She lived in Topeka, Kansas. Her home was five blocks from an elementary school. Because Linda was black and the students in that school were white, she had to attend a school for black children 21 blocks away. Her parents sued the school board of Topeka. They said their daughter was being unfairly discriminated against. They said the school system had violated her right to the equal protection of the laws.

The Browns' lawyer was Thurgood Marshall. Marshall later became the first black justice of the Supreme Court. He argued that segregated schools could **not** be equal. This time, the Supreme Court agreed. The Court said that requiring black children to attend separate schools denied them equal protection under the Fourteenth Amendment.

Ending discrimination

The Court's decision in this case did not end unfair discrimination by some states. Many states fought against the Court's order. The Governor of Arkansas tried to stop black students from entering an all-white high school. President Dwight Eisenhower ordered the U.S. Army to make sure the black students' rights to go to the school were protected.

How is the government protecting the rights of these students?

The Brown case dealt only with public schools. It did not protect blacks from other types of racial discrimination. In the 1960s, many blacks and whites worked to end other kinds of unfair treatment. Because of their efforts, many laws were passed against discrimination.

As blacks won these rights, other groups began to ask for them also. Women, Native Americans, Hispanics, disabled citizens, older citizens, and other groups have worked to gain equal protection for their rights.

Reviewing and using the lesson

1. Explain why the Linda Brown case was important. Did the Court's decision change the schools in your community?

2. Should people have the right to live wherever they choose, no matter what their race or religion might be? Why or why not?

3. Should the majority of the people in a community be able to say that people of a certain race, religion, or age cannot live in their community? Why or why not?

4. Should a person who is hiring someone have to give everyone an equal chance to get the job, no matter what their race, sex, or religion might be? Why or why not?

5. Is changing the Constitution or passing a law enough to end unfair discrimination? Do you and others have any responsibility to help end unfair discrimination? Explain your answer.

6. Explain these terms: Fourteenth Amendment, discrimination, equal protection.

How does the Constitution protect your right to be treated fairly by the government?

Purpose of Lesson

In the last lesson we looked at how the equal protection clause protects people from unfair discrimination. In this lesson we will look at other words in the Constitution that are about fairness. These words are in the due process clauses of the Constitution. We will see how these clauses help protect our lives, liberty, and property from unfair and unreasonable acts by our government.

What is due process of law?

The **right to due process** is the right to be treated fairly by your government. You will find the words **due process** in two places in our Constitution. They are in both the Fifth Amendment and the Fourteenth Amendment.

- **Fifth Amendment.** It says that no person shall be deprived of life, liberty, or property without **due process of law.** This amendment protects your right to be treated fairly by the **federal** government.

- **Fourteenth Amendment.** This amendment says that **state** governments cannot deprive you of your life, liberty, or property without **due process of law.** It protects your right to be treated fairly by your **state** and **local** governments.

Most people don't know that before the Fourteenth Amendment was passed, the Bill of Rights only protected you from unfair treatment by the federal government. The Fourteenth Amendment has been used to protect you from unfair treatment by state and local governments.

Due process means that members of your government must use fair methods or **procedures** when doing their jobs. They must use fair procedures when they gather information. They must use fair procedures when they make decisions. They must use fair procedures when they enforce the law.

For example, the Bill of Rights says that if you are accused of a crime, you have the right to have a lawyer help defend you. Suppose the government did not allow you to have a lawyer. The government would have violated your right to due process that is guaranteed by the Constitution.

Do you have a right to a lawyer even if you can't afford one?

What does the right to have a lawyer in a criminal case mean? Does it mean the government must pay for a lawyer to help you if you cannot afford to pay for one yourself? The Supreme Court has changed its ideas about this right over a period of years. In 1963, in a famous case, the Supreme Court thought again about what the constitutional right to a lawyer means.

Problem solving

When should you have the right to a lawyer?

Your class should be divided into small groups of three to five students. Each group should read the following case and answer the questions that follow it. Be prepared to explain your answers to the class.

Gideon v. Wainwright (1963)

Clarence Gideon was accused of breaking into a poolroom in Florida. Police said he had stolen a pint of wine and some coins from a cigarette machine. Gideon was a poor, uneducated man who was fifty years old. He did not know much about the law. However, he believed he could not get a fair trial without a lawyer to help him.

When Gideon appeared in court, he asked the judge to appoint a lawyer for him. He was too poor to hire one himself. The judge told him that he did not have the right to have a lawyer appointed for him unless he was charged with murder.

Gideon was tried before a jury, and he tried to defend himself. He made an opening speech to the jury and **cross-examined** the witnesses against him. He then called witnesses to **testify** for him and made a final speech to the jury. The jury decided he was guilty. Gideon was sent to the state prison to serve for five years.

---

cross-examine
to question witnesses testifying for the other side

testify
give information or evidence

126

From prison he wrote a petition to the Supreme Court. It was handwritten in pencil. He argued that all citizens have a right to a lawyer in cases where they might be sent to prison.

1. Should Gideon have been given a lawyer to help him? Why or why not?

2. Should the right to have a lawyer mean the government has to provide one to anyone who cannot afford to hire one? Why or why not?

3. Should lawyers be appointed to help people accused of breaking any laws, even traffic laws? Why or why not?

4. When should a person have the right to a lawyer? Upon arrest? Before being questioned? Before the trial? After the trial, if the person thinks the trial was unfair and wants another trial?

5. Should defendants have the right to have the services of other experts to help them prepare for their trials? Fingerprint experts? People to find witnesses? Psychiatrists?

Why is it important to protect your rights to due process?

Why is due process important in criminal trials?

To get some idea of the importance of fair procedures in enforcing the law, read the following situations. Then answer the questions that follow them. Suppose you lived in a country in which the following things could happen.

- If the police suspected you of a crime, they could force you by any means to give them information that might show you were guilty.

- If you were taken to court, the judge could use any means to get information from you to decide whether you were guilty.

- The leaders of the country could make decisions about your life, liberty, or property in secret, without allowing you or anyone else to participate.

1. Would you believe that you would be treated fairly if you were accused of a crime? Why or why not?

2. Even if you haven't broken the law or been arrested, would you want other people suspected of crimes treated in these ways? Why or why not?

3. Would you want decisions that affected your life, liberty, or property made in secret? Why or why not?

Other examples of due process rights

Due process means the right to be treated fairly by all agencies of your government. Your right to due process is not limited to making sure you are treated fairly by law enforcement agencies and the courts. The government must treat you fairly whenever it creates laws about your right to travel, raise a family, or use your property. It must also be fair if you apply for a government job or receive government benefits. The right to due process means the right to be treated fairly in all your dealings with your government.

Reviewing and using the lesson

1. Why is the guarantee of due process so important? Give examples to support your position.

2. Look at the Bill of Rights. Find parts of it that are designed to make sure you are treated fairly by your government. Be prepared to explain what you have found to your class.

3. Explain these terms: due process, procedures, cross-examine, testify.

LESSON 20

How does the Constitution protect your right to vote?

Purpose of Lesson

The Framers could not agree about who should have the right to vote. They left it up to the state governments to decide who could vote in each state. At the beginning of our nation, most state governments only allowed white men who owned land to vote. They did not allow blacks, women, and Native Americans to vote.

In this lesson, you will learn how people have fought to gain the right to vote. When you have completed this lesson, you should be able to tell how voting rights were gained by people who were denied them in the past.

Problem solving

Who should have the right to vote?

Your class should be divided into groups of about five students each. Each group should answer the questions that follow. Then a representative of each group should report its answers to the class.

1. Who should have the right to vote in elections for officials of your government? Who should not have this right? Explain your reasons.

2. Why should people have the right to vote for their government officials?

Early limits on the right to vote

The Framers let the state governments decide who could vote. Early in our nation's history, state governments usually just allowed white men with property to vote. They believed a person who owned property would be more likely to vote carefully than someone without property. They thought a person with property would have more to lose if a bad government came to power. In particular, a person with property would vote for people who would be careful to protect property. As you have learned, the Founders considered the protection of property to be one of the main purposes of government.

During the 50 years following the adoption of the Constitution, the vote was given to all white men. However, blacks, women, and Native Americans still could not vote. It took many years and much hard work before these groups gained the right to vote.

Gaining the right to vote for black men

Over 100 years ago, the Civil War ended slavery in America. Soon after the war, three amendments, called the **Civil War Amendments**, were passed. They were intended to give the newly freed slaves the rights of citizens.

- The **Thirteenth Amendment** abolished slavery.

- The **Fourteenth Amendment** made the newly freed slaves citizens of the United States.

- The **Fifteenth Amendment** said that states could not deny the right to vote to anyone because of race or color, or because that person had once been a slave.

Black men had gained the right to vote. However, these amendments did not stop states from trying to keep blacks from voting. In many Southern states, laws were passed to make it difficult or impossible for black men to vote. The following are examples of some of these laws.

- **Literacy tests.** Some states required people to take literacy tests in order to vote. These tests were difficult for most black men because they did not have a chance to get an education. The tests were also given unfairly so that even educated blacks would fail while whites who could not read would pass.

- **Grandfather clauses.** Some states made laws that allowed people who could not pass a literacy test to vote if their grandfathers had the right to vote. Whites could qualify because their grandfathers had the right to vote. However, no blacks could qualify because none of their grandfathers, who had been slaves, had been allowed to vote.

- **Poll taxes.** Some states charged a poll tax. Since most former slaves were very poor, they could not pay the tax and therefore could not vote.

People fought to get these laws changed. It took a long time. In 1915, the Supreme Court said that grandfather clauses in state laws were unconstitutional. However, as late as the 1960s, literacy tests and poll taxes were used to keep blacks from voting.

In the 1950s, more and more people began to demand that the rights of blacks be protected. Black and white people worked together to get unfair state laws changed. They gave speeches and participated in marches and demonstrations. These actions became known as the **civil rights movement.**

As a result of these efforts, the **Twenty-Fourth Amendment** was added to the Constitution in 1964. It says that the right of citizens to vote in national elections cannot be taken away for not paying a poll tax or any other tax. In 1966, the Supreme Court said this right also applied to state elections.

In 1965, Congress passed the **Voting Rights Act.** This new law further protected black people's right to vote. It forced the states to obey the Constitution.

Women gain the right to vote

For most of our history, women did not have the right to vote. Women were the largest group ever denied the right to vote in our nation.

Women began the national fight to gain the right to vote at a women's rights convention held in New York in 1848. At that convention, leaders such as Lucretia Mott and Elizabeth Cady Stanton argued that women should have equal rights with men. They said these rights could be protected only if women were allowed to vote.

In 1870, the Fifteenth Amendment gave black men the right to vote. Many women had fought for this amendment. They tried hard to win their own right to vote at the same time. However, many people then believed that a woman's place was in the home. They did not believe women should participate in their government. Such ideas hurt women's chances of winning the right to vote at that time.

The struggle for women's right to vote was a long and difficult one. Women picketed in front of the White House and marched in parades. Some women went to the polls and insisted on voting, even though people threw

rotten eggs at them. The famous women's leader, Susan B. Anthony, was arrested and fined $100 for voting illegally in 1872. She refused to pay the fine and the judge did not force her to. He said he did not want people to feel sorry for her.

By 1900, a few states allowed women to vote. There were even two women candidates for President, though most women still could not vote. In 1872, Victoria Woodhull was the first woman candidate for President. In 1884, Belva Lockwood, a well-known lawyer of the time, ran for President.

Women continued to fight and gain support. Finally, in 1920, the **Nineteenth Amendment** was added to the Constitution. It gave women the right to vote. One hundred thirty years after the Constitution was signed, women had won the right to vote. However, there are still very few women elected to the legislative or executive branches of our national government. For example, in 1988, out of 100 members of the Senate only two were women. Out of 435 members of the House of Representatives, only 23 were women.

Native Americans gain the right to vote

For over 130 years after the Constitution was written, most Native Americans were not citizens and did not have the right to vote. They were governed by treaties with the United States, by their tribal laws, and by special laws passed by Congress.

Native Americans finally were made citizens in 1924 by a law passed by Congress. They now have the right to vote in both state and federal elections.

Eighteen-year-olds gain the right to vote

In 1970 only four states let citizens younger than twenty-one years old vote. In that year, hundreds of thousands of young Americans had been drafted to fight in Vietnam. Many of them were under twenty-one, and they did not have the right to vote.

People argued that if eighteen-year-olds were old enough to be sent to Vietnam, they were old enough to vote. As a result, a law passed by Congress gave people eighteen and older the right to vote in national elections. In March, 1971, the **Twenty-Sixth Amendment** was added to the Constitution. It gave citizens eighteen years old and older the right to vote in all federal, state, and local elections.

People who fought for young people's right to vote believed they would use this right and participate in our government. However, today, fewer eighteen to twenty-one-year-olds vote than any other age group.

Voting requirements today

State governments still make some decisions about voting rights. For example, all states have passed laws saying that only citizens can vote. States also limit the right to vote to people who are residents of the state and who register to vote.

Some states deny the right to vote to people who have been found guilty of serious crimes.

The right to vote in a democracy is very important. Yet it is a right that has taken many citizens a long time and much hard work to achieve. It is also a right that often is not used.

When did each of these groups win the right to vote?

Reviewing and using the lesson

1. Explain how women won the right to vote. Why do you think women were not given the right to vote in the first place?

2. Why do you think there are so few women in Congress?

3. Why was the right to vote given to eighteen-year-olds? Why do you think the group between the ages of eighteen and twenty-one was the last to win the right to vote?

4. Why do you think fewer young people vote than older people?

5. Should people have to pass any kind of test before they can vote? For example, should they have to be able to speak, read, and write English? Why or why not?

6. Explain these terms: Civil War Amendments, literacy tests, grandfather clauses, poll taxes, civil rights movement.

Unit Five

What are the responsibilities of citizens?

You have learned about the history of our government and its Constitution. You know that it is the responsibility of members of the government to protect our rights. They are also responsible for promoting the welfare of everyone in our country.

There is an important question we have not yet studied. What are our responsibilities as citizens?

In our country, it is as important for citizens to do their job as it is for the government to do its job. In fact, the government cannot be a good government if the citizens are not good citizens.

What is a good citizen? What are the things citizens should do? What should we not do? We know that we have rights; do we also have responsibilities?

This unit will not tell you the answers to these questions. You must answer them yourselves. This unit will help you to decide what you ought to do as a citizen of the United States.

LESSON 21

What responsibilities accompany our rights?

Purpose of Lesson

Suppose your government does everything it can to protect your rights. Is this enough? Will your rights be protected? Do we have any responsibility to protect not only our own rights, but each other's as well?

In this lesson you will discuss some important questions about the responsibilities of citizens. You must develop your own answers to these questions. We hope this lesson will help you develop good answers.

Is a good constitution enough?

The Framers planned our government carefully. They organized it so its powers were limited. They separated the powers of our government among three different branches. They balanced the powers among these branches. They provided ways each branch could check or limit the powers of the other branches. Finally, they added a Bill of Rights. The Bill of Rights now protects our rights from unfair treatment by our national, state, and local governments.

Some of the Framers believed they had organized the government very well. They believed the way they planned the government was enough to make sure our rights and welfare would be protected.

Other Framers did not agree. They did agree that the way the government was organized was very important. However, they believed that the government would only work well if there were good people running it. They also believed it would only succeed if the citizens were good citizens.

Today, most people agree. A well-written constitution is not enough to protect our rights. We need to elect leaders who will make and enforce laws that protect our rights and promote our welfare.

However, even a good constitution and good leaders may not be enough. If we want to protect our rights and welfare, we, the people, have certain responsibilities to fulfill. Let's examine what some of these responsibilities might be.

What responsibilities go along with our rights?

Most of us agree we all should have certain basic rights. For example, we all want the right to speak freely. We want the right to believe as we wish. We also want to be able to own property and to travel wherever we want to go. Is it fair to say that if we want these rights, we must also take on some responsibilities? Let's examine this question.

Problem solving

Can you have rights without responsibilities?

In the last unit, you studied five of your basic rights. Let's examine what some of the responsibilities might be that go along with these rights. Your class should be divided into five groups. Each group should develop answers to the questions on one of the rights listed below. Then each group should report its findings to the class.

Group 1. Freedom of expression. Your government cannot unfairly limit your right to speak freely. What responsibilities might go along with this right?

- Suppose you attend a meeting of students in your school. The group is supposed to suggest rules for the playground. You have the right to speak and give your suggestions. What responsibilities should you have in the way you speak and in what you say? List and explain these responsibilities.

- What responsibilities should other students at the meeting have toward your right to speak? List and explain these responsibilities.

- What responsibilities should you have toward the other students' right to speak? List and explain these responsibilities.

- What might happen to the right to free speech if no one fulfilled the responsibilities you have discussed?

What responsibilities do you have to protect freedom of speech?

140

Group 2. *Freedom of religion.* Your government cannot interfere with your right to believe as you wish. It cannot unfairly limit your right to practice your religious beliefs. What responsibilities might go along with these rights?

- Suppose you believe in a particular religion. You attend a church or temple in your community. List and explain what responsibilities you should have in the way you practice your religious beliefs.

- Suppose there are people in your community who believe in different religions or in no religion at all. List and explain what responsibilities they should have to protect your right to practice your religious beliefs.

- List and explain what responsibilities you should have to protect other people's right to practice their religious beliefs or not to have any religious beliefs.

- What might happen to the right of freedom of religion if no one fulfilled the responsibilities you have discussed?

What are your responsibilities to protect people's right to believe as they wish?

What responsibilites do you have to treat everyone equally?

Group 3. The right to be treated equally. Your government may not favor some people over others because of such things as their age, sex, race, or religion. What responsibilities might go along with this right?

- Suppose people in your community are planning a picnic for the public. List and explain what responsibilities they might have to be fair to you no matter what your age, sex, race, or religion may be.

- Suppose you were helping to plan the picnic. List and explain what responsibilities you think you should have to other people no matter what their age, sex, race, or religion might be.

- What might happen to the right to be treated equally if no one fulfilled the responsibilities you have discussed?

What responsibilities do you have to treat other people fairly?

Group 4. The right to be treated fairly by your government. Your government must be fair to you when it is gathering information and making decisions. What responsibilities might go along with this right?

- Suppose someone has accused you of doing something wrong in your school or community. What responsibilities should that person have toward you? List and explain those responsibilities.

- Suppose you have accused others of doing something wrong in your school or community. What responsibilities should you have toward them? List and explain those responsibilities.

- What might happen to the right to be treated fairly if no one fulfilled the responsibilities you have discussed?

What responsibilities go along with your right to vote?

Group 5. The right to vote and run for public office.
When you are eighteen, you will have the right to vote. You will also have the right to run for public office if you want to. What responsibilities might go along with this right?

- Suppose you are about to vote in an election. You can vote for or against five proposed laws. You must choose between two people running for Congress. What responsibilities should you have? List and explain those responsibilities.

- Suppose some friends, neighbors, and others in your community do not agree with the way you are going to vote. List and explain what responsibilities they have toward your right to vote.

- Suppose you do not agree with the way some of your friends, neighbors, and others in your community are going to vote. List and explain what responsibilities you should have toward their right to vote.

- What might happen to the right to vote if no one fulfilled the responsibilities you have discussed?

Reviewing and using the lesson

1. Explain what you think are some of the most important responsibilities you have in order to protect your rights.

2. What responsibilities should you take to protect the rights of others? Why?

How can we promote the common welfare?

Purpose of Lesson

In the last lesson, we discussed what responsibilities we have to protect our rights. In this final lesson, we will look at the responsibilities we all might have to promote our common welfare. We will also look at ways we can participate in making decisions about what is best for everyone.

How do we decide what is best for everyone?

We elect members of government to promote our welfare. Do we, the people, also have a responsibility to promote the common welfare? Do we have a responsibility to promote not only our own interests, but each other's as well?

Most people would agree there are times when we should put the common welfare above our own personal interests. Sometimes it is easy to agree on what is best for everyone. We agree we must keep armed forces to protect ourselves. We know everyone needs an opportunity to go to school. Everyone needs to be able to earn a living. We all agree that everyone should have a place to live and enough to eat.

Sometimes it is not so easy to agree upon what is best for everyone. Sometimes we need to be able to make difficult decisions about what is the best thing to do.

Problem solving

What decision would you reach?

Your class should be divided into small groups of three to five students. Each group should read the following situation and answer the questions which follow it. Then, each group should report its answers to the class.

Suppose you live in a small community. Most of the people in your community work in a large factory. The smoke from the factory pollutes the air in your community so much it is dangerous to everyone's health. It also pollutes the air of nearby communities.

It would be very expensive to buy machinery to stop the pollution. Owners of the factory say they cannot afford to buy it and still stay in business. If the factory closed, many people in your community would lose their jobs. There are no other jobs available in the community.

What do you think is the best solution to this problem ?

146

> **What should be done?**
>
> 1. What is the problem that has to be solved?
>
> 2. What are some different ways to solve the problem?
>
> 3. What are the advantages and disadvantages of each solution you have suggested?
>
> 4. What do you think is the best solution? Give the reasons for your choice.

How important is it for you to participate in your government?

Our government is a government of the people, by the people, and for the people. You are a part of the people. We, the people, run our government. We elect people to work for us in our government.

We need to be sure they do a good job. If they do, we will vote for them again. If they do not, we may want to vote for others to take their place. We participate in government to protect our rights and our welfare.

You cannot vote until you are eighteen. However, you can still participate in our government. One of the most important things you can do is something you have already started to do. You can learn something about our government. You can learn what it is supposed to do. You can learn how it works. You can learn what rights you have. And, finally, you can think about what responsibilities you should take.

Thomas Jefferson and other important Founders thought all people should have an opportunity to get an education. They thought the main purpose of education should be to prepare you to become a thoughtful and responsible citizen. They knew our government can only work well if the people are well educated.

Jefferson said, "if a nation expects to be ignorant and free, it expects what never was and what never will be."

You can also participate by keeping informed about what your government is doing. You can keep informed by reading newspapers and magazines, and by listening to the news on radio and television. You can talk about what your government is doing with your parents and friends. If there is a law or problem you feel strongly about, you can express your opinion. You can tell your friends and you can write to members of your government.

How can you participate in your government?

You can partipate by volunteering to help people in your community. You can participate by taking part in the government of your classroom and your school. You can start now to be an informed and effective citizen.

What responsibilities will you fulfill?

You have learned a great deal about our nation's government. You have learned about the government's responsibilities and your rights. You have also discussed some of the responsibilities of citizens.

You have inherited a free society. It is your society. You are free to make many choices. You are free to choose what kind of citizen you want to be.

You can help keep your society free. You can help make sure all people's rights are protected. You can help promote our common welfare.

We hope this book helps you make a wise decision about what kind of citizen you want to be.

Reviewing and using the lesson

1. How can schools help students become good citizens?

2. What are some ways you can participate in your government now?

3. Does a good citizen have a responsibility to try to improve the lives of people who need help? Why or why not?

4. What responsibilities should a citizen take to protect or promote the welfare of people in other countries? Explain your position.

Reference Section

Declaration of Independence

IN CONGRESS, JULY 4, 1776.

A DECLARATION

BY THE **REPRESENTATIVES** OF THE

UNITED STATES OF AMERICA,

IN GENERAL CONGRESS ASSEMBLED

WHEN in the Course of human Events, it becomes necessary for one People to dissolve the Political Bands which have connected them with another, and to assume among the Powers of the Earth, the separate and equal Station to which the Laws of Nature and of Nature's God entitle them, a decent Respect to the Opinions of Mankind requires that they should declare the causes which impel them to the Separation.

We hold these Truths to be self-evident, that all Men are created equal, that they are endowed by their Creator with certain unalienable Rights, that among these are Life, Liberty, and the Pursuit of Happiness--That to secure these Rights, Governments are instituted among Men, deriving their just Powers from the Consent of the Governed, that whenever any Form of Government becomes destructive of these Ends it is the Right of the People to alter or to abolish it, and to institute new Government, laying its Foundation on such Principles, and organizing its Powers in such Form, as to them shall seem most likely to effect their Safety and Happiness. Prudence, indeed, will dictate that Governments long established should not be changed for light and transient Causes; and accordingly all Experience hath shewn, that Mankind are more disposed to suffer, while Evils are sufferable, than to right themselves by abolishing the Forms to which they are accustomed. But when a long Train of Abuses and Usurpations, pursuing invariably the same Object, evinces a Design to reduce them under absolute Despotism, it is their Right, it is their Duty, to throw off such Government, and to provide new Guards for their future Security. Such has been the patient Sufferance of these Colonies; and such is now the Necessity which constrains them to alter their former Systems of Government. The History of the present King of Great-Britain is a History of repeated Injuries and Usurpations, all having in direct Object the Establishment of an absolute Tyranny over these States. To prove this, let Facts be submitted to a candid World.

He has refused his Assent to Laws, the most wholesome and necessary for the public Good.

He has forbidden his Governors to pass Laws of immediate and pressing Importance, unless suspended in their Operation till his Assent should be obtained; and when so suspended, he has utterly neglected to attend to them.

He has refused to pass other Laws for the Accommodation of large Districts of People, unless those People would relinquish the Right of Representation in the Legislature, a Right inestimable to them, and formidable to Tyrants only.

He has called together Legislative Bodies at Places unusual, uncomfortable, and distant from the Depository of their public Records, for the sole Purpose of fatiguing them into Compliance with his Measures.

He has dissolved Representative Houses repeatedly, for opposing with manly Firmness his Invasions on the Rights of the People.

He has refused for a long Time, after such Dissolutions, to cause others to be elected; whereby the Legislative Powers, incapable of Annihilation, have returned to the People at large for their exercise; the State remaining in the mean time exposed to all the Dangers of Invasions from without, and Convulsions within.

He has endeavored to prevent the Population of these States; for that Purpose obstructing the Laws for Naturalization of Foreigners; refusing to pass others to encourage their Migrations hither, and raising the Conditions of new Appropriations of Lands.

He has obstructed the Administration of Justice, by refusing his Assent to Laws for establishing Judiciary Powers.

He has made Judges dependent on his Will alone, for the Tenure of their Offices, and the Amount and Payment of their Salaries.

He has erected a Multitude of new Offices, and sent hither Swarms of Officers to harass our People and eat out their Substance.

He has kept among us, the Times of Peace, Standing Armies, without the consent of our Legislatures.

He has affected to render the Military independent of and superior to the Civil Power.

He has combined with others to subject us to a Jurisdiction foreign to our Constitution, and unacknowledged by our Laws; giving his Assent to their Acts of pretended Legislation:

For quartering large Bodies of Armed Troops among us:

For protecting them, by a mock Trial, from Punishment for any Murders which they should commit on the Inhabitants of these States:

For cutting off our Trade with all Parts of the World:

For imposing Taxes on us without our Consent:

For depriving us, in many Cases, of the Benefits of Trial by Jury:

For transporting us beyond Seas to be tried for pretended Offenses:

For abolishing the free System of English Laws in a neighbouring Province, establishing therein an Arbitrary Government, and enlarging its Boundaries, so as to render it at once an Example and fit Instrument for introducing the same absolute Rule into these Colonies:

For taking away our Charters, abolishing our most valuable Laws, and altering fundamentally the Forms of our Governments:

For suspending our own Legislatures, and declaring themselves invested with Power to legislate for us in all Cases whatsoever.

He has abdicated Government here, by declaring us out of his Protection and waging War against us.

He has plundered our Seas, ravaged our Coasts, burnt our Towns, and destroyed the Lives of our People.

He is, at this Time, transporting large Armies of foreign Mercenaries to compleat the Works of Death, Desolation, and Tyranny, already begun with circumstances of Cruelty and Perfidy, scarcely paralleled in the most barbarous Ages, and totally unworthy the Head of a civilized Nation.

He has constrained our fellow Citizens taken Captive on the high Seas to bear Arms against their Country, to become the Executioners of their Friends and Brethren, or to fall themselves by their Hands.

He has excited domestic Insurrections amongst us, and has endeavoured to bring on the Inhabitants of our Frontiers, the merciless Indian Savages, whose known Rule of Warfare, is an undistinguished Destruction, of all Ages, Sexes and Conditions.

In every stage of these Oppressions we have Petitioned for Redress in the most humble Terms: Our repeated Petitions have been answered only by repeated Injury. A Prince, whose Character is thus marked by every act which may define a Tyrant, is unfit to be the Ruler of a free People.

Nor have we been wanting in Attentions to our British Brethren. We have warned them from Time to Time of Attempts by their Legislature to extend an unwarrantable Jurisdiction over us. We have reminded them of the Circumstances of our Emigration and Settlement here. We have appealed to their native Justice and Magnanimity, and we have conjured them by the Ties of our common Kindred to disavow these Usurpations, which, would inevitably interrupt our Connections and Correspondence. They too have been deaf to the Voice of Justice and of Consanguinity. We must, therefore, acquiesce in the Necessity, which denounces our Separation, and hold them, as we hold the rest of Mankind, Enemies in War, in Peace, Friends.

We, therefore, the Representatives of the UNITED STATES OF AMERICA, in GENERAL CONGRESS, Assembled, appealing to the Supreme Judge of the World for the Rectitude of our Intentions, do, in the Name, and by Authority of the good People of these Colonies, solemnly Publish and Declare, That these United Colonies are, and of Right ought to be, FREE AND INDEPENDENT STATES; that they are absolved from all Allegiance to the British Crown, and that all political Connection between them and the State of Great-Britain, is and ought to be totally dissolved; and that as FREE AND INDEPENDENT STATES, they have full Power to levy War, conclude Peace, contract Alliances, establish Commerce, and to do all other Acts and Things which INDEPENDENT STATES may of right do. And for the support of this Declaration, with a firm Reliance on the Protection of divine Providence, we mutually pledge to each other our Lives, our Fortunes, and our sacred Honor.

Signed by ORDER and in BEHALF of the CONGRESS,

JOHN HANCOCK, PRESIDENT.

Signers of the Declaration of Independence

New-Hampshire
Josiah Bartlett,
Wm. Whipple,
Matthew Thornton.

Massachusetts-Bay
Saml. Adams,
John Adams,
Robt. Treat Paine,
Elbridge Gerry.

Rhode-Island and Providence, &c.
Step. Hopkins,
William Ellery.

Connecticut
Roger Sherman,
Saml. Huntington,
Wm. Williams,
Oliver Wolcott.

New-York
Wm. Floyd,
Phil. Livingston,
Frans. Lewis,
Lewis Morris.

New-Jersey
Richd. Stockton,
Jno. Witherspoon,
Fras. Hopkinson,
John Hart,
Abra. Clark.

Pennsylvania
Robt. Morris,
Benjamin Rush,
Benja. Franklin,
John Morton,
Geo. Clymer,
Jas. Smith,
Geo. Taylor,
James Wilson,
Geo. Ross.

Delaware
Casar Rodney,
Geo. Read,
(Tho M:Kean.)

Maryland
Samuel Chase,
Wm. Paca,
Thos. Stone,
Charles Carroll, of Carrollton.

Virginia
George Wythe,
Richard Henry Lee,
Ths. Jefferson,
Benja. Harrison,
Thos. Nelson, Jr.
Francis Lightfoot Lee,
Carter Braxton.

North-Carolina
Wm. Hooper,
Joseph Hewes,
John Penn.

South-Carolina
Edward Rutledge,
Thos. Heyward, Junr.
Thomas Lynch, Junr.
Arthur Middleton.

Georgia
Button Gwinnett,
Lyman Hall,
Geo. Walton.

According to the authenticated list printed by order of Congress of January 18, 1777.
Spelling, and abbreviations of names conform to original printed list.

The Constitution of the United States of America

Preamble

We the People of the United States, in Order to form a more perfect Union, establish Justice, insure domestic tranquility, provide for the common defence, promote the general Welfare, and secure the Blessings of Liberty to ourselves and our Posterity, do ordain and establish this Constitution for the United States of America.

ARTICLE I.

The Legislative Branch

Section 1.

All legislative Powers herein granted shall be vested in a Congress of the United States, which shall consist of a Senate and House of Representatives.

Section 2.

House of Representatives: Organization and Power of Impeachment

1. The House of Representatives shall be composed of Members chosen every second Year by the People of the several States, and the Electors in each State shall have the Qualifications requisite for Electors of the most numerous Branch of the State Legislature.

2. No Person shall be a Representative who shall not have attained to the Age of twenty five Years, and been seven Years a Citizen of the United States, and who shall not, when elected, be an Inhabitant of that State in which he shall be chosen.

3. [Representatives and direct Taxes shall be apportioned among the several States which may be included within this Union, according to their respective Numbers, which shall be determined by adding to the whole Number of free Persons, including those bound to Service for a Term of Years, and excluding Indians not taxed, three fifths of all other Persons.]* The actual Enumeration shall be made within three Years after the first Meeting of the Congress of the United States, and within every subsequent Term of ten Years, in such Manner as they shall by Law direct. The number of Representatives shall not exceed one for every thirty Thousand, but each State shall have at Least one Representative; and until such enumeration shall be made, the State of New Hampshire shall be entitled to choose three, Massachusetts eight, Rhode Island and Providence Plantations one, Connecticut five, New York six, New Jersey four, Pennsylvania eight, Delaware one, Maryland six, Virginia ten, North Carolina five, South Carolina five, and Georgia three.

4. When vacancies happen in the Representation from any State, the Executive Authority thereof shall issue Writs of Election to fill such Vacancies.

5. The House of Representatives shall choose their Speaker and other Officers; and shall have the sole Power of Impeachment.

Section 3.

The Senate, Organization and Powers of Impeachment

1. The Senate of the United States shall be composed of two Senators from each State, [chosen by the Legislature

---

* Changed by section 2 of the Fourteenth Amendment.

thereof,]* for six Years; and each Senator shall have one Vote.

2. Immediately after they shall be assembled in Consequence of the first Election, they shall be divided as equally as may be into three Classes. The seats of the Senators of the first Class shall be vacated at the Expiration of the second Year, of the second Class at the Expiration of the fourth Year, and of the third Class at the Expiration of the sixth Year, so that one third may be chosen every second Year; [and if Vacancies happen by Resignation, or otherwise, during the Recess of the Legislature of any State, the Executive thereof may make temporary Appointments until the next Meeting of the Legislature, which shall then fill such Vacancies.]*

3. No Person shall be a Senator who shall not have attained to the Age of thirty Years, and been nine Years a Citizen of the United States, and who shall not, when elected, be an Inhabitant of that State for which he shall be chosen.

4. The Vice President of the United States shall be President of the Senate, but shall have no Vote, unless they be equally divided.

5. The Senate shall choose their other officers, and also a President pro tempore, in the Absence of the Vice President, or when he shall exercise the Office of President of the United States.

6. The Senate shall have the sole Power to try all Impeachments. When sitting for that Purpose, they shall be on Oath or Affirmation. When the President of the United States is tried, the Chief Justice shall preside: And no person shall be convicted without the Con-

currence of two thirds of the Members present.

7. Judgment in Cases of Impeachment shall not extend further than to removal from Office, and disqualification to hold and enjoy any Office of honor, Trust or Profit under the United States; but the Party convicted shall nevertheless be liable and subject to Indictment, Trial, Judgment and Punishment, according to Law.

Section 4.
Elections and Meeting of Congress

1. The Times, Places and Manner of holding Elections for Senators and Representatives shall be prescribed in each State by the Legislature thereof; but the Congress may at any time by Law make or alter such Regulations, except as to the Places of choosing Senators.

2. The Congress shall assemble at least once in every Year, and such Meeting shall be [on the first Monday in December,]** unless they shall by Law appoint a different Day.

Section 5.
Congress's Rules of Procedure, Powers, Quorum, Journals, Meetings, Adjournments

1. Each House shall be the Judge of the Elections, Returns and Qualifications of its own Members, and a Majority of each shall constitute a Quorum to do Business; but a smaller Number may adjourn from day to day, and may be authorized to compel the Attendance of absent Members, in such Manner, and under such Penalties as each House may provide.

2. Each House may determine the Rules of its Proceedings, punish its members for disorderly Behavior, and,

---

* Changed by the Seventeenth Amendment.
** Changed by section 2 of the Twentieth Amendment.

with the Concurrence of two thirds, expel a Member.

3. Each House shall keep a Journal of its Proceedings, and from time to time publish the same, excepting such Parts as may in their Judgment require Secrecy; and the Yeas and Nays of the Members of either House on any question shall, at the Desire of one fifth of those Present, be entered on the Journal.

4. Neither House, during the Session of Congress, shall, without the Consent of the other, adjourn for more than three days, nor to any other Place than that in which the two Houses shall be sitting.

Section 6.
Pay, Privileges, Limitations

1. The Senators and Representatives shall receive a Compensation for their Services, to be ascertained by Law, and paid out of the Treasury of the United States. They shall in all cases, except Treason, Felony and Breach of the Peace, be privileged from Arrest during their Attendance at the Session of their respective Houses, and in going to and returning from the same; and for any Speech or Debate in either House, they shall not be questioned in any other Place.

2. No Senator or Representative shall, during the Time for which he was elected, be appointed to any civil Office under the Authority of the United States, which shall have been created, or the Emoluments whereof shall have been increased during such time; and no Person holding any Office under the United States, shall be a Member of either House during his Continuance in Office.

Section 7.
Procedure in Passing Bills, President's Veto Power

1. All Bills for raising Revenue shall originate in the House of Representatives; but the Senate may propose or concur with Amendments as on other Bills.

2. Every Bill which shall have passed the House of Representatives and the Senate, shall, before it becomes a Law, be presented to the President of the United States; if he approve he shall sign it, but if not he shall return it, with his Objections, to that House in which it shall have originated, who shall enter the Objections at large on their Journal, and proceed to reconsider it. If after such Reconsideration two thirds of that House shall agree to pass the Bill, it shall be sent, together with the Objections, to the other House, by which it shall likewise be reconsidered, and if approved by two thirds of that House, it shall become a Law. But in all such Cases the Votes of both Houses shall be determined by yeas and nays, and the Names of the Persons voting for and against the Bill shall be entered on the Journal of each House respectively. If any Bill shall not be returned by the President within ten Days (Sundays excepted) after it shall have been presented to him, the Same shall be a Law, in like Manner as if he had signed it, unless the Congress by their Adjournment prevent its Return, in which Case it shall not be a Law.

3. Every Order, Resolution, or Vote to which the Concurrence of the Senate and House of Representatives may be necessary (except on a question of Adjournment) shall be presented to the

President of the United States; and before the Same shall take Effect, shall be approved by him, or being disapproved by him, shall be repassed by two thirds of the Senate and House of Representatives, according to the Rules and Limitations prescribed in the Case of a Bill.

Section 8.
Powers Delegated to Congress

The Congress shall have Power

1. To lay and collect Taxes, Duties, Imposts and Excises, to pay the Debts and provide for the common Defence and general Welfare of the United States; but all Duties, Imposts and Excises shall be uniform throughout the United States;

2. To borrow Money on the credit of the United States;

3. To regulate Commerce with foreign Nations, and among the several States, and with the Indian Tribes;

4. To establish an uniform Rule of Naturalization, and uniform Laws on the subject of Bankruptcies throughout the United States;

5. To coin Money, regulate the Value thereof, and of Foreign Coin, and fix the Standard of Weights and Measures;

6. To provide for the Punishment of counterfeiting the Securities and current Coin of the United States;

7. To establish Post Offices and post Roads;

8. To promote the Progress of Science and useful Arts, by securing for limited Times to Authors and Inventors the exclusive Right to their respective Writings and Discoveries;

9. To constitute Tribunals inferior to the supreme Court;

10. To define and punish Piracies and Felonies committed on the high Seas, and Offenses against the Law of Nations;

11. To declare War, grant Letters of Marque and Reprisal, and make Rules concerning Captures on Land and Water;

12. To raise and support Armies, but no Appropriation of Money to that Use shall be for a longer Term than two Years;

13. To provide and maintain a Navy;

14. To make Rules for the Government and Regulation of the land and naval Forces;

15. To provide for calling forth the Militia to execute the Laws of the Union, suppress Insurrections and repel Invasions;

16. To provide for organizing, arming, and disciplining the Militia, and for governing such Part of them as may be employed in the Service of the United States, reserving to the States respectively, the Appointment of the Officers, and the Authority of training the Militia according to the discipline prescribed by Congress;

17. To exercise exclusive Legislation in all Cases whatsoever, over such District (not exceeding ten Miles square) as may, by Cession of particular States, and the Acceptance of Congress, become the Seat of the Government of the United States, and to exercise like Authority over all Places purchased by the Consent of the Legislature of the State in which the Same shall be, for the Erection of Forts, Magazines, Arsenals, dock-Yards and other needful Buildings; — And

18. To make all Laws which shall be necessary and proper for carrying into Execution the foregoing powers, and all other Powers vested by this Constitution in the Government of the United States, or in any Department or Officer thereof.

Section 9.
Powers Denied to Congress

1. The Migration or Importation of such Persons as any of the States now existing shall think proper to admit, shall not be prohibited by the Congress prior to the Year one thousand eight hundred and eight, but a Tax or duty may be imposed on such Importation, not exceeding ten dollars for each Person.

2. The Privilege of the Writ of Habeas Corpus shall not be suspended, unless when in Cases of Rebellion or Invasion the public Safety may require it.

3. No Bill of Attainder or ex post facto Law shall be passed.

4. [No Capitation, or other direct, Tax shall be laid, unless in Proportion to the Census or Enumeration herein before directed to be taken.]*

5. No Tax or Duty shall be laid on Articles exported from any State.

6. No Preference shall be given by any Regulation of Commerce or Revenue to the Ports of one State over those of another: nor shall Vessels bound to, or from, one State, be obliged to enter, clear, or pay Duties in another.

7. No Money shall be drawn from the Treasury, but in Consequence of Appropriations made by Law; and a regular Statement and Account of the Receipts and Expenditures of all public Money shall be published from time to time.

8. No Title of Nobility shall be granted by the United States: And no Person holding any Office of Profit or Trust under them, shall, without the Consent of the Congress, accept of any present, Emolument, Office, or Title, of any kind whatever, from any King, Prince, or foreign State.

Section 10.
Restrictions on States' Powers

1. No State shall enter into any Treaty, Alliance, or Confederation; grant Letters of Marque and Reprisal; coin Money; emit Bills of Credit; make any Thing but gold and silver Coin a Tender in Payment of Debts; pass any Bill of Attainder, ex post facto Law, or Law impairing the Obligation of Contracts, or grant any Title of Nobility.

2. No State shall, without the Consent of the Congress, lay any Imposts or Duties on Imports or Exports, except what may be absolutely necessary for executing its inspection Laws: and the net Produce of all Duties and Imposts, laid by any State on Imports or Exports, shall be for the Use of the Treasury of the United States; and all such Laws shall be subject to the Revision and Control of the Congress.

3. No State shall, without the Consent of Congress, lay any Duty of Tonnage, keep Troops, or Ships of War in time of Peace, enter into any Agreement or Compact with another State, or with a foreign Power, or engage in War, unless actually invaded, or in such imminent Danger as will not admit of delay.

---

* Changed by the Sixteenth Amendment.

ARTICLE II.

The Executive Branch

Section 1.

President and Vice-President: Election, Qualifications, and Oath

1. The executive Power shall be vested in a President of the United States of America. He shall hold his Office during the term of four Years, and, together with the Vice President, chosen for the same Term, be elected, as follows.

2. Each State shall appoint, in such Manner as the Legislature thereof may direct, a Number of Electors, equal to the whole Number of Senators and Representatives to which the State may be entitled in the Congress: but no Senator or Representative, or Person holding an Office of Trust or Profit under the United States, shall be appointed an Elector.

3. [The Electors shall meet in their respective states, and vote by Ballot for two Persons, of whom one at least shall not be an Inhabitant of the same State with themselves. And they shall make a List of all the Persons voted for, and of the Number of Votes for each; which List they shall sign and certify, and transmit sealed to the Seat of the Government of the United States, directed to the President of the Senate. The President of the Senate shall, in the Presence of the Senate and House of Representatives, open all the Certificates, and the Votes shall then be counted. The Person having the greatest Number of Votes shall be the President, if such Number be a Majority of the whole Number of Electors appointed; and if there be more than one who have such Majority, and have an equal Number of Votes, then the House of Representatives shall immediately choose by Ballot one of them for President; and if no Person have a Majority, then from the five highest on the List the said House shall in like manner choose the President. But in choosing the President, the Votes shall be taken by States, the Representation from each State having one Vote; A quorum for this Purpose shall consist of a Member or Members from two thirds of the States, and a Majority of all the States shall be necessary to a Choice. In every Case, after the Choice of the President, the Person having the greatest Number of Votes of the Electors shall be the Vice President. But if there should remain two or more who have equal Votes, the Senate shall choose from them by Ballot the Vice President.]*

4. The Congress may determine the Time of choosing the Electors, and the day on which they shall give their Votes; which Day shall be the same throughout the United States.

5. No Person except a natural born Citizen, or a Citizen of the United States at the time of the Adoption of this Constitution, shall be eligible to the Office of the President; neither shall any person be eligible to that Office who shall not have attained to the Age of thirty five Years, and been fourteen Years a Resident within the United States.

6. [In Case of the Removal of the President from Office, or of his Death, Resignation, or Inability to discharge the Powers and Duties of the said Office, the Same shall devolve on the Vice President, and the Congress may by Law provide for the Case of Removal, Death, Resignation or Inability, both of the President and Vice President,

---

* Changed by the Twelfth Amendment.

160

declaring what Officer shall then act as President, and such Officer shall act accordingly, until the Disability be removed, or a President shall be elected.]*

7. The President shall, at stated Times, receive for his Services, a Compensation, which shall neither be increased nor diminished during the Period for which he shall have been elected, and he shall not receive within that Period any other Emolument from the United States, or any of them.

8. Before he enter the Execution of his Office, he shall take the following Oath or Affirmation: —"I do solemnly swear (or affirm) that I will faithfully execute the Office of President of the United States, and will to the best of my Ability, preserve, protect, and defend the Constitution of the United States."

Section 2.
Powers of the President

1. The President shall be Commander in Chief of the Army and Navy of the United States, and of the Militia of the several States, when called into the actual Service of the United States; he may require the Opinion, in writing, of the principal Officer in each of the executive Departments, upon any Subject relating to the Duties of their respective Offices, and he shall have Power to grant Reprieves and Pardons for Offenses against the United States, except in Cases of Impeachment.

2. He shall have Power, by and with the Advice and Consent of the Senate, to make Treaties, provided two thirds of the Senators present concur; and he shall nominate, and by and with the Advice and Consent of the Senate, shall appoint Ambassadors, other public Mini-

sters and Consuls, Judges of the supreme Court, and all other Officers of the United States, whose Appointments are not herein otherwise provided for, and which shall be established by Law: but the Congress may by Law vest the Appointment of such inferior Officers, as they think proper, in the President alone, in the Courts of Law, or in the Heads of Departments.

3. The President shall have Power to fill up all Vacancies that may happen during the Recess of the Senate, by granting Commissions which shall expire at the End of their next Session.

Section 3.
Duties of the President

He shall from time to time give to the Congress Information of the State of the Union, and recommend to their Consideration such Measures as he shall judge necessary and expedient; he may, on extraordinary Occasions, convene both Houses, or either of them, and in Case of Disagreement between them, with Respect to the Time of Adjournment, he may adjourn them to such Time as he shall think proper; he shall receive Ambassadors and other public Ministers; he shall take Care that the Laws be faithfully executed, and shall Commission all the Officers of the United States.

Section 4.
Impeachment and Removal from Office for Crimes

The President, Vice President and all civil Officers of the United States, shall be removed from Office on Impeachment for, and Conviction of, Treason, Bribery, or other high Crimes and Misdemeanors.

*   Changed by the Twenty-Fifth Amendment.

ARTICLE III.

The Judicial Branch

Section 1.

Federal Courts, Tenure of Office

The judicial Power of the United States, shall be vested in one supreme Court, and in such inferior Courts as the Congress may from time to time ordain and establish. The Judges, both of the supreme and inferior Courts, shall hold their Offices during good Behavior, and shall, at stated Times, receive for their Services a Compensation, which shall not be diminished during their Continuance in Office.

Section 2.

Jurisdiction of Federal Courts

1. The judicial Power shall extend to all Cases, in Law and Equity, arising under this Constitution, the Laws of the United States, and Treaties made, or which shall be made, under their Authority; — to all Cases affecting Ambassadors, other public Ministers and Consuls; — to all Cases of admiralty and maritime Jurisdiction; — to Controversies to which the United States shall be a Party; — to Controversies between two or more States; [between a State and Citizens of another State;]* between Citizens of different States; — between Citizens of the same State claiming Lands under Grants of different States; — [and between a State, or the Citizens thereof, and foreign States, Citizens or Subjects.]*

2. In all Cases affecting Ambassadors, other public Ministers and Consuls, and those in which a State shall be Party, the supreme Court shall have original Jurisdiction. In all the other Cases before mentioned, the supreme Court shall have appellate Jurisdiction, both as to Law and Fact, with such Ex-

* Changed by the Eleventh Amendment.

ceptions, and under such Regulations as the Congress shall make.

3. The Trial of all Crimes, except in Cases of Impeachment, shall be by Jury; and such Trial shall be held in the State where said Crimes shall have been committed; but when not committed within any State, the Trial shall be at such Place or Places as the Congress may by Law have directed.

Section 3.

Treason: Conviction Of and Punishment For

1. Treason against the United States shall consist only in levying War against them, or in adhering to their Enemies, giving them Aid and Comfort. No Person shall be convicted of Treason unless on the Testimony of two Witnesses to the same overt Act, or on Confession in open Court.

2. The Congress shall have Power to declare the Punishment of Treason, but no Attainder of Treason shall work Corruption of Blood, or Forfeiture except during the Life of the Person attainted.

ARTICLE IV.

Relations Among the States

Section 1.

Full Faith and Credit

Full Faith and Credit shall be given in each State to the public Acts, Records, and judicial Proceedings of every other State; And the Congress may by general Laws prescribe the manner in which such Acts, Records and Proceedings shall be proved, and the Effect thereof.

Section 2.

Rights of State Citizens; Right of Extradition

1. The Citizens of each State shall be entitled to all Privileges and Im-

munities of Citizens in the several States.

2. A Person charged in any State with Treason, Felony, or other Crime, who shall flee from Justice, and be found in another State, shall on Demand of the executive Authority of the State from which he fled, be delivered up, to be removed to the State having Jurisdiction of the Crime.

3. [No person held to Service or Labour in one State, under the Laws thereof, escaping into another, shall, in Consequence of any Law or Regulation therein, be discharged from such Service or Labour, but shall be delivered up on Claim of the Party to whom such Service or Labour may be due.]*

Section 3.
Admission of New States

1. New States may be admitted by the Congress into this Union; but no new State shall be formed or erected within the Jurisdiction of any other State; nor any State be formed by the Junction of two or more States, or parts of States, without the Consent of the Legislatures of the States concerned as well as of the Congress.

2. The Congress shall have Power to dispose of and make all needful Rules and Regulations respecting the territory or other Property belonging to the United States; and nothing in this Constitution shall be so construed as to Prejudice any Claims of the United States, or of any particular State.

Section 4.
Republican Government Guaranteed

The United States shall guarantee to every State in this Union a Republican Form of Government, and shall protect each of them against Invasion; and on

Application of the Legislature, or of the Executive (when the Legislature cannot be convened) against domestic Violence.

ARTICLE V.
Amendment Procedures

The Congress, whenever two thirds of both Houses shall deem it necessary, shall propose Amendments to this Constitution, or, on the Application of the Legislatures of two thirds of the several States, shall call a Convention for proposing Amendments, which, in either Case, shall be valid to all Intents and Purposes, as Part of this Constitution, when ratified by the Legislatures of three fourths of the several States, or by Conventions in three fourths thereof, as the one or the other Mode of Ratification may be proposed by the Congress; Provided that no Amendment which may be made prior to the Year One thousand eight hundred and eight shall in any Manner affect the first and fourth Clauses in the Ninth Section of the first Article; and that no State, without its Consent, shall be deprived of its equal Suffrage in the Senate.

ARTICLE VI.
Supremacy of the Constitution and Federal Laws

1. All debts contracted and Engagements entered into, before the Adoption of this Constitution, shall be as valid against the United States under this Constitution, as under the Confederation.

2. This Constitution, and the Laws of the United States which shall be made in Pursuance thereof; and all Treaties made, or which shall be made, under the Authority of the United States, shall be the supreme Law of the Land; and the Judges in every State

* Changed by the Thirteenth Amendment.

under the Authority of the United States, shall be the supreme Law of the Land; and the Judges in every State shall be bound thereby, any Thing in the Constitution or Laws of any State to the Contrary notwithstanding.

3. The Senators and Representatives before mentioned, and the Members of the several State Legislatures, and all executive and judicial Officers, both of the United States and of the several States, shall be bound by Oath or Affirmation, to support this Constitution; but no religious Test shall ever be required as a Qualification to any Office or public Trust under the United States.

ARTICLE VII.

Ratification

The Ratification of the Conventions of nine States, shall be sufficient for the Establishment of this Constitution between the States so ratifying the Same.

Done in Convention by the unanimous consent of the States present the seventeenth day of September in the year of our Lord one thousand seven hundred and eighty seven and of the Independence of the United States of America the Twelfth. In witness whereof we have hereunto subscribed our Names,

George Washington—President and deputy from Virginia

This constitution was adopted on September 17, 1787 by the Constitutional Convention, and was declared ratified on July 2, 1788.

Signers of the Constitution

New Hampshire

John Langdon

Nicholas Gilman

Massachusetts

Nathaniel Gorham

Rufus King

Connecticut

William Samuel Johnson

Roger Sherman

New York

Alexander Hamilton

New Jersey

William Livingston

David Brearley

William Paterson

Jonathan Dayton

Pennsylvania

Benjamin Franklin

Thomas Mifflin

Robert Morris

George Clymer

Thomas Fitzsimons

Jared Ingersoll

James Wilson

Gouverneur Morris

Delaware

George Read

Gunning Bedford, Jr.

John Dickinson

Richard Bassett

Jacob Broom

Maryland

James McHenry

Daniel of St. Tho. Jenifer

Daniel Carrol

Virginia

John Blair

James Madison, Jr.

North Carolina

William Blount

Richard Dobbs Spaight

Hugh Williamson

South Carolina

John Rutledge

Charles Cotesworth Pinckney

Charles Pinckney

Pierce Butler

Georgia

William Few

Abraham Baldwin

Attest *William Jackson*
Secretary

Amendments to the Constitution

Since 1787, twenty-six amendments have been proposed by the Congress and ratified by the several states, pursuant to the fifth Article of the original Constitution.

Amendment I.

Freedom of Religion and Expression

Congress shall make no law respecting an establishment of religion, or prohibiting the free exercise thereof; or abridging the freedom of speech, or of the press, or the right of the people peaceably to assemble, and to petition the Government for a redress of grievances. (Ratified December, 1791.)

Amendment II.

Right to Bear Arms

A well regulated Militia, being necessary to the security of a free State, the right of the people to keep and bear Arms, shall not be infringed. (Ratified December, 1791.)

Amendment III.

Quartering of Soldiers

No Soldier shall, in time of peace be quartered in any house, without the consent of the Owner, nor in time of war, but in a manner to be prescribed by law. (Ratified December, 1791.)

Amendment IV.

Security From Unreasonable Searches and Seizures

The right of the people to be secure in their persons, houses, papers, and effects, against unreasonable searches and seizures, shall not be violated, and no Warrants shall issue, but upon probable cause, supported by Oath or affirmation, and particularly describing the place to be searched, and the persons or things to be seized. (Ratified December, 1791.)

Amendment V.

Rights of Due Process of Law

No person shall be held to answer for a capital, or otherwise infamous crime, unless on a presentment or indictment of a Grand Jury, except in cases arising in the land or naval forces, or in the Militia, when in actual service in time of War or public danger; nor shall any person be subject for the same offence to be twice put in jeopardy of life or limb, nor shall be compelled in any criminal case to be a witness against himself, nor be deprived of life, liberty, or property, without due process of law; nor shall private property be taken for public use without just compensation. (Ratified December, 1791.)

Amendment VI.

Right to a Fair Trial

In all criminal prosecutions, the accused shall enjoy the right to a speedy and public trial, by an impartial jury of the State and district wherein the crime shall have been committed; which district shall have been previously ascertained by law, and to be informed of the nature and cause of the accusation; to be confronted with the witnesses against him; to have compulsory process for obtaining witnesses in his favor, and to have the assistance of counsel for his defence. (Ratified December, 1791.)

Amendment VII.

Trial by Jury

In Suits at common law, where the value in controversy shall exceed twenty dollars, the right of trial by jury shall be preserved, and no fact tried by a jury shall be otherwise re-examined in any Court of the United States, than according to the rules of the common law. (Ratified December, 1791.)

Amendment VIII.

Fair Bail and Punishments

Excessive bail shall not be required, nor excessive fines imposed, nor cruel and unusual punishments inflicted. (Ratified December, 1791.)

Amendment IX.

Rights Retained by the People

The enumeration in the Constitution of certain rights shall not be construed to deny or disparage others retained by the people. (Ratified December, 1791.)

Amendment X.

Powers Reserved to States and People

The powers not delegated to the United States by the Constitution, nor prohibited by it to the States, are reserved to the States respectively, or to the people. (Ratified December, 1791.)

Amendment XI.

Limitations on Federal Courts

The Judicial power of the United States shall not be construed to extend to any suit in law or equity, commenced or prosecuted against one of the United States by Citizens of another State, or by Citizens or Subjects of any Foreign State. (Ratified February, 1795.)

Amendment XII.

Election of President

The Electors shall meet in their respective states, and vote by ballot for President and Vice President, one of whom, at least, shall not be an inhabitant of the same state with themselves; they shall name in their ballots the person voted for as President, and in distinct ballots the person voted for as Vice-President, and they shall make distinct lists of all persons voted for as President, and of all persons voted for as Vice-President, and of the number of votes for each, which lists they shall sign and certify, and transmit sealed to the seat of the government of the United States, directed to the President of the Senate; — The President of the Senate shall, in the presence of the Senate and House of Representatives, open all the certificates and the votes shall then be counted; — The person having the greatest number of votes for President, shall be the President, if such number be a majority of the whole number of Electors appointed; and if no person have such majority, then from the persons having the highest numbers not exceeding three on the list of those voted for as President, the House of Representatives shall choose immediately, by ballot, the President. But in choosing the President, the votes shall be taken by states, the representation from each state having one vote; a quorum for this purpose shall consist of a member or members from two-thirds of the states, and a majority of all the states shall be necessary to a choice. [And if the House of Representatives shall not choose a President whenever the right of choice shall devolve upon them, before the fourth day of March next following, then the Vice-President shall act as President, as in the case of the death or other constitutional disability of the President —]* The person having the greatest number of votes as Vice-President, shall be the Vice-President, if such number be a majority of the whole number of Electors appointed, and if no person have a majority, then from the two highest numbers on the list, the Senate shall choose the Vice-President; a quorum for the purpose shall consist of

---

* Superseded by section 3 of the Twentieth Amendment.

two-thirds of the whole number of Senators, and a majority of the whole number shall be necessary to a choice. But no person constitutionally ineligible to the office of President shall be eligible to that of Vice-President of the United States. (Ratified June, 1804.)

Amendment XIII.

Slavery Abolished

Section 1. Neither slavery nor involuntary servitude, except as a punishment for crime whereof the party shall have been duly convicted, shall exist within the United States, or any place subject to their jurisdiction.

Section 2. Congress shall have power to enforce this article by appropriate legislation. (Ratified December, 1865.)

Amendment XIV.

Equal Protection and Due Process; Citizenship Defined and Guaranteed

Section 1. All persons born or naturalized in the United States and subject to the jurisdiction thereof, are citizens of the United States and of the State wherein they reside. No State shall make or enforce any law which shall abridge the privileges or immunities of citizens of the United States; nor shall any State deprive any person of life, liberty, or property, without due process of law; nor deny to any person within its jurisdiction the equal protection of the laws.

Section 2. Representatives shall be apportioned among the several States according to their respective numbers, counting the whole number of persons in each State, excluding Indians not taxed. But when the right to vote at any election for the choice of electors for President and Vice President of the United States, Representatives in Congress, the Executive and Judicial officers of a State, or the members of the Legislature thereof, is denied to any of the male inhabitants of such State, being twenty-one years of age, and citizens of the United States, or in any way abridged, except for participation in rebellion, or other crime, the basis of representation therein shall be reduced in the proportion which the number of such male citizens shall bear to the whole number of male citizens twenty-one years of age in such State.

Section 3. No person shall be a Senator or a Representative in Congress, or elector of President and Vice President, or hold any office, civil or military, under the United States, or under any State, who, having previously taken an oath, as a member of Congress, or as an officer of the United States, or as a member of any State legislature, or as an executive or judicial officer of any State, to support the Constitution of the United States, shall have engaged in insurrection or rebellion against the same, or given aid or comfort to the enemies thereof. But Congress may by a vote of two-thirds of each House, remove such disability.

Section 4. The validity of the public debt of the United States, authorized by law, including debts incurred for payment of pensions and bounties for services in suppressing insurrection or rebellion, shall not be questioned. But neither the United States nor any State shall assume or pay any debt or obligation incurred in aid of insurrection or rebellion against the United States, or any claim for the loss or emancipation of any slave; but all such debts, obligations and claims shall be held illegal and void.

Section 5. The Congress shall have power to enforce, by appropriate legislation, the provisions of this article. (Ratified July, 1868.)

Amendment XV.

Blacks' Right to Vote

Section 1. The right of citizens of the United States to vote shall not be denied or abridged by the United States or by any State on account of race, color, or previous condition of servitude.

Section 2. The Congress shall have power to enforce this article by appropriate legislation. (Ratified February, 1870.)

Amendment XVI.

Power to Tax Incomes

The Congress shall have power to lay and collect taxes on incomes, from whatever source derived, without apportionment among the several States, and without regard to any census or enumeration. (Ratified February, 1913.)

Amendment XVII.

Popular Election of Senators

The Senate of the United States shall be composed of two Senators from each State, elected by the people thereof, for six years; and each Senator shall have one vote. The electors in each State shall have the qualifications requisite for electors of the most numerous branch of the State legislatures.

When vacancies happen in the representation of any State in the Senate, the executive authority of such State shall issue writs of election to fill such vacancies: Provided, That the legislature of any State may empower the executive thereof to make temporary appointments until the people fill the vacancies by election as the legislature may direct.

This amendment shall not be so construed as to affect the election or term of any Senator chosen before it becomes valid as part of the Constitution. (Ratified April, 1913.)

Amendment XVIII.

Prohibition of Alcoholic Beverages

[Section 1. After one year from the ratification of this article the manufacture, sale, or transportation of intoxicating liquors within, the importation thereof into, or the exportation thereof from the United States and all territory subject to the jurisdiction thereof for beverage purposes is hereby prohibited.

Section 2. The Congress and the several States shall have concurrent power to enforce this article by appropriate legislation.

Section 3. This article shall be inoperative unless it shall have been ratified as an amendment to the Constitution by the legislatures of the several States, as provided in the Constitution, within seven years from the date of the submission hereof to the States by the Congress.]* (Ratified January, 1919.)

Amendment XIX.

Female Suffrage

The right of citizens of the United States to vote shall not be denied or abridged by the United States or by any State on account of sex.

Congress shall have power to enforce this article by appropriate legislation. (Ratified August, 1920.)

Amendment XX.

Changes in Terms of President and Congress

Section 1. The terms of the President and Vice President shall end at

---

* Repealed by the Twenty-First Amendment.

noon on the 20th day of January, and the terms of Senators and Representatives at noon on the 3d day of January, of the years in which such terms would have ended if this article had not been ratified; and the terms of their successors shall then begin.

Section 2. The Congress shall assemble at least once in every year, and such meeting shall begin at noon on the 3d day of January, unless they shall by law appoint a different day.

Section 3. If, at the time fixed for the beginning of the term of the President, the President elect shall have died, the Vice President elect shall become President. If a President shall not have been chosen before the time fixed for the beginning of his term, or if the President elect shall have failed to qualify, then the Vice President elect shall act as President until a President shall have qualified; and the Congress may by law provide for the case wherein neither a President elect nor a Vice President elect shall have qualified, declaring who shall then act as President, or the manner in which one who is to act shall be selected, and such person shall act accordingly until a President or Vice President shall have qualified.

Section 4. The Congress may by law provide for the case of the death of any of the persons from whom the House of Representatives may choose a President whenever the right of choice shall have devolved upon them, and for the case of the death of any of the persons from whom the Senate may choose a Vice President whenever the right of choice shall have devolved upon them.

Section 5. Sections 1 and 2 shall take effect on the 15th day of October following the ratification of this article.

Section 6. This article shall be inoperative unless it shall have been ratified as an amendment to the Constitution by the legislatures of three-fourths of the several States within seven years from the date of its submission. (Ratified January, 1933.)

Amendment XXI.
Repeal of Alcohol Prohibition

Section 1. The eighteenth article of amendment to the Constitution of the United States is hereby repealed.

Section 2. The transportation or importation into any State, Territory, or possession of the United States for delivery or use therein of intoxicating liquors, in violation of the laws thereof, is hereby prohibited.

Section 3. This article shall be inoperative unless it shall have been ratified as an amendment to the Constitution by conventions in the several States, as provided in the Constitution, within seven years from the date of the submission hereof to the States by the Congress. (Ratified December, 1933.)

Amendment XXII.
President Limited to Two Terms

Section 1. No person shall be elected to the office of the President more than twice, and no person who has held the office of President, or acted as President, for more than two years of a term to which some other person was elected President shall be elected to the office of the President more than once. But this Article shall not apply to any person holding the office of President when this Article was proposed by the Congress, and shall not prevent any person who may be holding the office of President, or acting as President, during the term within which this Article becomes operative from holding the office of President or acting as President during the remainder of such term.

Section 2. This article shall be inoperative unless it shall have been ratified as an amendment to the Constitution by the legislatures of three-fourths of the several States within seven years from the date of its submission to the States by the Congress. (Ratified February, 1951.)

Amendment XXIII.

Presidential Suffrage for District of Columbia

Section 1. The District constituting the seat of Government of the United States shall appoint in such manner as the Congress may direct:

A number of electors of President and Vice President equal to the whole number of Senators and Representatives in Congress to which the District would be entitled if it were a State, but in no event more than the least populous State; they shall be in addition to those appointed by the States, but they shall be considered, for the purposes of the election of President and Vice President, to be electors appointed by a State; and they shall meet in the District and perform such duties as provided by the twelfth article of amendment.

Section 2. The Congress shall have power to enforce this article by appropriate legislation. (Ratified March, 1961.)

Amendment XXIV.

Poll Tax Forbidden

Section 1. The right of citizens of the United States to vote in any primary or other election for President or Vice President, for electors for President or Vice President, or for Senator or Representative in Congress, shall not be denied or abridged by the United States or any State by reason of failure to pay any poll tax or other tax.

Section 2. The Congress shall have power to enforce this article by appropriate legislation. (Ratified January, 1964.)

Amendment XXV.

Procedures for Presidential Succession

Section 1. In case of the removal of the President from office or of his death or resignation, the Vice President shall become President.

Section 2. Whenever there is a vacancy in the office of the Vice President, the President shall nominate a Vice President who shall take office upon confirmation by a majority vote of both Houses of Congress.

Section 3. Whenever the President transmits to the President pro tempore of the Senate and the Speaker of the House of Representatives his written declaration that he is unable to discharge the powers and duties of his office, and until he transmits to them a written declaration to the contrary, such powers and duties shall be discharged by the Vice President as Acting President.

Section 4. Whenever the Vice President and a majority of either the principal officers of the executive departments or of such other body as Congress may by law provide, transmit to the President pro tempore of the Senate and the Speaker of the House of Representatives their written declaration that the President is unable to discharge the powers and duties of his office, the Vice President shall immediately assume the powers and duties of the office as Acting President.

Thereafter, when the President transmits to the President pro tempore of the Senate and the Speaker of the

House of Representatives his written declaration that no inability exists, he shall resume the powers and duties of his office unless the Vice President and a majority of either the principal officers of the executive department or of such other body as Congress may by law provide, transmit within four days to the President pro tempore of the Senate and the Speaker of the House of Representatives their written declaration that the President is unable to discharge the powers and duties of his office. Thereupon Congress shall decide the issue, assembling within forty-eight hours for that purpose if not in session. If the Congress, within twenty-one days after receipt of the latter written declaration, or, if Congress is not in session, within twenty-one days after Congress is required to assemble, determines by two-thirds vote of both Houses that the President is unable to discharge the powers and duties of his office, the Vice President shall continue to discharge the same as Acting President; otherwise, the President shall resume the powers and duties of his office. (Ratified February, 1967.)

Amendment XXVI.

Voting Age Lowered to Eighteen

Section 1. The right of citizens of the United States, who are eighteen years of age or older, to vote shall not be denied or abridged by the United States or by any State on account of age.

Section 2. The Congress shall have power to enforce this article by appropriate legislation. (Ratified July, 1971.)

This is the original text and section numbers. Descriptive headings have been added by editors. Passages in brackets indicate that they were changed by Amendments.

Biographies of Important Framers

Dickinson, John (1732-1808)
Dickinson was born in Maryland. He was the son of a wealthy farm family. He was educated by private tutors and then studied law in Philadelphia and London. He set up his first law practice in Philadelphia, where he served in the Pennsylvania legislature. Dickinson became famous all over the colonies for opposing British taxation. He served in the Continental Army. He headed the committee that wrote the Articles of Confederation. By 1786, he believed the Articles needed to be changed. Dickinson was highly respected. He made important contributions to the Philadelphia Convention but left early because of illness. He spent his later years writing about politics.

Ellsworth, Oliver (1745-1807)
Ellsworth was a member of a rich Connecticut family. He graduated from the College of New Jersey. He taught school and served as a minister before going into law. He was soon considered one of Connecticut's best lawyers. Ellsworth served in the Continental Congress. He did not want the national government to become too strong. He also did not want the people to be given too much power. Ellsworth did not sign the Constitution, although he later became Chief Justice of the Supreme Court.

Franklin, Benjamin (1706-1790)
Franklin was the oldest delegate to the Philadelphia Convention. He was one of the best-known men in America. Born into a poor family, Franklin became an inventor, scientist, diplomat, and publisher. He served as an ambassador to England and France and as governor of Pennsylvania. At the convention, Franklin was a compromiser. He sometimes brought the delegates together by making them laugh. He played an important role in creating the Great Compromise. He favored a strong national government and argued that the Framers should trust the judgment of the people. Although he was in poor health in 1787, he missed few—if any—sessions. He was carried to and from the meeting place in a special chair. Although he did not agree with everything in the Constitution, he believed that no other convention could come up with a better document.

Gerry, Elbridge (1744-1814)
Gerry was born into a wealthy family in Massachusetts. He attended Harvard, learning politics from Samuel Adams, a revolutionary leader. Gerry protested against British policies and signed the Declaration of Independence. Gerry often changed his mind about political issues. For example, after Shays' Rebellion, he spoke against giving the common people too much power. But he still argued for yearly elections and against giving the Senate, which was not elected by the people, too much power. Gerry refused to sign the Constitution and worked against ratification. Throughout his life, he served in a variety of offices. He died in 1814 while serving as Vice President.

Hamilton, Alexander (1755-1804)
Alexander Hamilton was one of the brightest delegates at the Philadelphia Convention. He was born in the British West Indies. As a young man, he traveled to New York City, where he attended

college until the American Revolution. He was very active in the war, serving as an aide to George Washington. Afterwards, he studied law and entered law practice. He served in the Continental Congress and was one of the leaders in calling for a constitutional convention. As a delegate, he played a rather small role because he had to miss many sessions. He wanted a much stronger national government than did most of the other delegates. Hamilton worked hard for ratification in New York. He served in Washington's government as Secretary of the Treasury. In 1804, Hamilton was killed in a duel with Aaron Burr.

Madison, James (1751-1836)

James Madison is often called the "Father of the Constitution." He was born to a wealthy family in Virginia. He was taught at home and in private schools. He graduated from the College of New Jersey. While debating whether to become a lawyer or minister, Madison became involved in the American Revolution. In 1780, Madison was chosen to serve in the Continental Congress, where he played an important role. He was one of the most influential people calling for a constitutional convention. He came to the Philadelphia Convention with a plan for the new government. Madison took extensive notes at the convention and spoke more than 150 times. He also worked hard on several committees. Madison was a key figure in the battle for ratification. Following the convention, he served as a member of the U.S. House of Representatives, helping to write the Bill of Rights and organize the executive department. Under Jefferson, Madison served as Secretary of State. He then followed Jefferson as President. In retirement, Madison continued to speak out on public issues.

Martin, Luther (1748-1826)

Luther Martin was born in New Jersey around 1748. After graduating from the College of New Jersey, he taught school and studied the law. He moved to Maryland, where he began practicing law. He served as state attorney general and in the Continental Congress. At the convention, he was against increasing the power of the federal government. Because he believed in the rights of the states and of the people, Martin wanted each state to have an equal vote in Congress. He also wanted a bill of rights. Although he owned six slaves, Martin opposed slavery and spoke out against it. Martin left the convention and did not sign the Constitution. He fought against ratification in Maryland. Martin served almost 30 years as Maryland state attorney general.

Mason, George (1725-1792)

George Mason was born into a wealthy Virginia family. He studied law and lived on a large plantation near George Washington's home. For most of his life, Mason stayed out of public office. He did serve in the Virginia legislature but quit in 1769. At the Philadelphia Convention, Mason spoke often. He argued against giving the President too much power and for a bill of rights. He also spoke against slavery, although at his death, he owned 300 slaves himself. Mason did not sign the Constitution and fought against ratification. He died shortly after the ratification of the Bill of Rights.

Morris, Gouverneur (1752-1816)

Morris was born in New York to a wealthy family. Early in life, he lost a leg in a carriage accident. He graduated from King's College in New York City and then studied law. Many of his family and friends were Loyalists, but Morris sided with the Patriots. He served in the state militia as well as in the New York legislature and the Continental Congress. When he was defeated for Congress in 1779, Morris moved to Philadelphia to practice law. At the Philadelphia Convention, Morris gave more speeches than anyone else. He favored a strong national government ruled by the upper classes. He served on many committees and was the primary writer of the actual document. After the convention, Morris spent ten years in Europe. He served briefly in the Senate, but then retired.

Pinckney, Charles (1757-1824)

Charles Pinckney was born in South Carolina, the son of a rich lawyer and planter. Pinckney trained as a lawyer. He served in the militia during the American Revolution, was captured by the British, and was a prisoner until 1781. He served in the Continental Congress and the South Carolina legislature. At the Philadelphia Convention, Pinckney spoke often. He was a good speaker who helped create the compromises that made the Constitution possible. After the convention, he held a variety of offices, including governor and U.S. senator. He worked to give the vote to all white males.

Randolph, Edmund (1753-1813)

Randolph was born into a well-known Virginia family of lawyers. He attended William and Mary College and then studied law under his father. The Revolution split the family. Edmund's father, mother, and two sisters were Loyalists while Edmund and his uncle were Patriots. Randolph served in the Continental Congress and as governor of Virginia. He gave the first major speech at the Philadelphia Convention, in which he criticized the Articles of Confederation. As leader of the Virginia delegation, he presented the Virginia Plan to the convention. Although the Constitution included many ideas similar to those in the Virginia Plan, he did not sign the document. However, George Washington persuaded Randolph to support ratification. Randolph served as Attorney General and Secretary of State under Washington.

Rutledge, John (1739-1800)

Rutledge was born in South Carolina and was taught at home — by his father and a tutor. He then studied law in London. He returned to South Carolina, where he practiced law and built a fortune. He was active in South Carolina politics in the 1760s and 1770s, serving in the Continental Congress and as governor. When the British seized Charleston, Rutledge had to flee to North Carolina. He gathered a force to recapture South Carolina. At the Philadelphia Convention, he was an important delegate, speaking often and well. He argued for the interests of the Southern states. Washington appointed Rutledge to the U.S. Supreme Court, where he served a brief time. He returned to South Carolina to serve on the state supreme court. In 1795, Washington again appointed him to the Supreme Court, this time as Chief Justice. The Senate rejected his nomination. He retired from public life after this defeat.

Sherman, Roger (1721-1793)

Born in 1721 in Massachusetts, Sherman spent most of his boyhood helping his father with farming and shoe-making chores. He read in whatever spare time he could find. In 1743, he moved to Connecticut, buying a store and entering politics. Sherman served in the state legislature and the Continental Congress, worked as a judge, and wrote essays and almanacs. He was one of the members of the committee that wrote the Declaration of Independence and the Articles of Confederation. Sherman attended nearly every session of the Philadelphia Convention and helped create the Great Compromise. He also worked hard to get Connecticut to ratify the Constitution. He later served in the House of Representatives and Senate.

Washington, George (1732-1798)
George Washington was born in Virginia. He grew up there on several plantations along the Potomac and Rapahannock Rivers. In 1753, he began his service to his country. It continued throughout his life, although he would rather have lived as a simple farmer. Washington's efforts as commander of the Continental Army are well known. After the Revolution, Washington returned to his home, Mount Vernon. At first he did not want to attend the Philadelphia Convention. His friends convinced him that he should. He was elected president of the convention, but spoke little. Nearly everyone thought that Washington would be the first President of the United States. He was, serving from 1788-1796. When he died, Washington's will said that his slaves should be freed when his wife Martha died.

Wilson, James (1741-1798)
Wilson was born and educated in Scotland. He arrived in America in 1765. He taught and studied law and set up a legal practice in Pennsylvania. He was active in the revolutionary effort, voting for independence and signing the Declaration. After the war, he defended Loyalists and their sympathizers. This action made many people in Pennsylvania angry. But by the 1780s, Wilson was again elected to the Continental Congress. Wilson was an important delegate to the Philadelphia Convention. He spoke even more often than Madison. Wilson led the ratification effort in Pennsylvania. He was appointed to the Supreme Court.

Yates, Robert (1738-1801)
Yates was born and educated in New York. He became a lawyer and set up practice in Albany. He served in several offices, spending the greatest amount of time as a justice of the New York Supreme Court (1777-1798). Yates left the Philadelphia Convention because he believed it had gone beyond its instructions from Congress. He worked against ratification. Yates kept notes of the parts of the convention he attended. These notes have been useful to historians.

Glossary

amendment. A change in or addition to a document.

American Revolution. The American colonies' war for independence from Great Britain. It took place from 1775 to 1781.

Articles. The major parts of the Constitution.

Articles of Confederation. The first constitution of the United States. It was adopted in 1781 and replaced in 1788 by our present Constitution.

basic rights. The rights to life, liberty, and property which everyone should have.

bill. A proposed law sent to the legislature for approval.

Bill of Rights. The first ten amendments to the Constitution. It contains the basic rights which the federal government may not interfere with.

board of inquiry. A group formed to study or investigate a situation.

Brown v. Board of Education. The 1954 Supreme Court case that decided that segregated schools were unconstitutional. The Court said that separate schools denied black children the equal protection of the laws.

cabinet. A group made up of the heads of the departments of the executive branch. They advise the President.

capital punishment. Death as a legal punishment for a crime; also called the death penalty.

checks and balances. The sharing and balancing of power among different branches of government so no one branch can completely control the others.

Chief Justice. The head of a court. The Chief Justice of the United States is head of the Supreme Court.

citizen. A person who is a member of a nation.

Civil War. The war between the Northern and Southern states that took place in our country between 1861-1865.

Civil War Amendments. The Thirteenth, Fourteenth, and Fifteenth Amendments to the Constitution passed after the Civil War. These amendments were intended to give the newly-freed slaves the rights of citizens.

civic virtue. Putting the common welfare above individual interests.

clause. A phrase in the Constitution.

colony. A settlement or territory ruled by another country.

common defense. Protection of the people from enemies.

common welfare. The good of the community as a whole.

compromise. A way to settle differences by each side agreeing to give up part of what it wants.

conflict. Disagreement; argument.

Congress. The national legislature of the United States. Congress has two houses, the Senate and the House of Representatives.

consent. To agree.

constitution. A set of rules and laws that tells how a government is organized and run.

constitutional government. A government in which the powers of the ruler or rulers are limited by a constitution. The rulers must obey the constitution.

Continental Congress. The national legislature which governed the American colonies from 1774 until the adoption of the Articles of Confederation.

convention. A formal assembly or meeting.

cross-examine. To question witnesses testifying for the other side in a trial.

Declaration of Independence. The statement which gave the reasons why the colonists wanted to free themselves from British rule. It was signed by the members of Congress on July 4, 1776.

delegate. A person picked to act for or represent others, usually at a convention or meeting.

democracy. A form of government in which power is held by the people. The people exercise their power either directly or through elected representatives.

dictator. A head of government who has unlimited power.

dictatorial government. A government in which the rulers have unlimited power.

discrimination. Unfair treatment of people because of their race, religion, or sex.

diversity. Having people of many different backgrounds.

domestic tranquility. As used in the Preamble, this phrase means a peaceful situation within our country.

due process. The right to be protected from unfair government procedures and laws.

enforce. To make people obey the law.

equal protection. Treating all individuals or groups of people equally under the law.

establishment clause. The part of the First Amendment that says the government cannot set up an official religion.

executive. The person who has power to carry out, or enforce, the law.

executive branch. The branch of government that carries out the laws made by the legislative branch.

federal system. A form of government in which power is divided between a central government and state and local governments.

Founders. The people who were important in the establishment of the United States.

Framers. The delegates to the Philadelphia Convention of 1787.

free exercise clause. The part of the First Amendment which says the government shall not deny a person the right to practice his religion.

freedom of expression. The freedoms of speech, press, assembly, and petition that are protected by the First Amendment.

freedom of religion. The right to hold whatever religious beliefs we wish without interference by the government.

fugitive slave clause. The part of the Constitution which said that slaves who escaped must be returned to their owners.

general welfare. The good of all the people.

government. The organization through which political authority is used.

grandfather clause. The law that allowed whites who could not pass a literacy test to vote if their grandfathers had been able to vote.

Great Compromise. The plan accepted at the Philadelphia Convention that called for Congress to have two houses. The Senate would have two senators from each state. In the House of Representatives, the number of representatives from each state would be based on its population.

hearing. A meeting in which citizens give their views to public officials.

House of Representatives. One house of Congress. The number of representatives from each state is based on its population.

immigrant. A person who leaves his or her native land to settle in another country.

impeach. To accuse a public official of committing a crime while he or she is in office.

indentured servant. A person who agreed to work for someone for a set period of time in return for the cost of coming to America.

interests. Those things which are to one's advantage or benefit.

interpret. To explain the meaning of something.

judicial branch. The branch of government that interprets and applies the laws and settles disputes.

judicial review. The power of the courts to say the Constitution does not allow the government to do something.

Judiciary Act of 1789. The law that established the federal court system below the Supreme Court.

justices. Members of the Supreme Court.

law. A bill that has been passed by the legislature and signed by the executive.

legislative branch. The branch of government that makes the laws.

liberty. Freedom.

limits. Restrictions; boundaries.

literacy tests. Tests given to people to prove they are able to read and write. These tests were used in the South to keep black people from voting.

Loyalists. Americans who supported Great Britain during the Revolution.

majority. More than half.

national government. The organization having political authority in a nation.

natural rights. The rights to life, liberty, and property.

Northwest Ordinance of 1787. An important law passed by Congress under the Articles of Confederation. The law provided for settling the western lands and organizing new states.

participation. Taking part in or sharing in the activities of a group or organization.

Patriots. Those Americans who supported the war for independence against Great Britain.

persecute. To cause suffering to a person or group because of their beliefs.

petition. A formal, written request.

Philadelphia Convention. The meeting held in Philadelphia in 1787 at which the U.S. Constitution was written.

plantation. A large farm usually found in the Southern states.

politics. The activities of getting and holding public office and making laws.

poll tax. A tax that voters in many states had to pay before they could vote.

population. The number of people living in an area.

Preamble. The introduction to the Constitution. In the Preamble, the Framers (1) stated that the people established the government, and (2) listed the purposes of the government.

procedures. The methods or steps taken to accomplish something.

property. Something that is owned.

ratify. Approve.

ratification. The formal approval of the Constitution by the states.

ratifying conventions. Meetings held in the states to approve the Constitution.

representatives. People elected to act for others.

republican government. A government in which power is held by the people who elect representatives to run the government for the common welfare.

responsibility. Duty or obligation.

retire. To leave a job upon reaching a certain age.

secretaries. The heads of the departments in the executive branch who act as advisers to the President.

segregation. The separation of people in schools and other public places because of their race.

self-sufficient. Able to provide most of one's own needs.

Senate. One house of Congress. Each state has two members in the Senate.

separation of powers. The division of powers among the different branches of government. In the United States, powers are divided among the legislative, executive, and judicial branches.

slavery. Ownership of human beings as property.

Supreme Court. The highest court in the United States.

testify. Give information or evidence, as at a hearing or trial.

three-fifths clause. The part of the Constitution that counted each slave as three-fifths of a person to determine how many representatives a state would have in Congress.

trade. The buying and selling of goods.

treaty. An official agreement between two or more governments or rulers.

unconstitutional. Not allowed by the Constitution; illegal.

veto. The power of the President to refuse to approve a bill passed by Congress.

witness. A person who is called to give evidence before a court.

Index

L

legislative branch 78
Locke, John 20
Lockwood, Belva 134
Loyalists 39

M

Madison, James 53, 54, 114
Marshall, Thurgood 122
Maryland 60, 97, 98
Massachusetts 47, 48, 60, 107, 113
Mott, Lucretia 133

N

national government 3, 5, 42-44, 47, 49, 51, 54, 55, 58, 59, 67, 75, 76, 81, 99, 100-102, 104
Native Americans 7, 10, 53, 65, 123, 130, 131, 134
natural rights 16, 20, 33, 38, 39, 41
Nineteenth Amendment 134
Northwest Ordinance 45, 49

P

Paine, Thomas 55
Philadelphia Convention 50, 52, 53, 54, 57, 58, 69
poll taxes 132, 136
Preamble to the Constitution 70, 71
President 1, 2, 27, 28, 78, 79, 83, 86, 88-94, 96, 97, 122, 134

R

republican government 21, 22, 24, 25
Rhode Island 53, 60, 113
Roman Republic 21